Q-Squared

Q-Squared

Combining Qualitative and
Quantitative Approaches
in Poverty Analysis

Paul Shaffer

OXFORD
UNIVERSITY PRESS

OXFORD

UNIVERSITY PRESS

Great Clarendon Street, Oxford, OX2 6DP,
United Kingdom

Oxford University Press is a department of the University of Oxford.
It furthers the University's objective of excellence in research, scholarship,
and education by publishing worldwide. Oxford is a registered trade mark of
Oxford University Press in the UK and in certain other countries

First Edition published in 2013
Impression: 1

British Library Cataloguing in Publication Data
Data available

Library of Congress Cataloging in Publication Data
Data available

ISBN 978–0–19–967690–3 (Hbk.)
ISBN 978–0–19–967691–0 (Pbk.)

Printed in Great Britain by
CPI Group (UK) Ltd, Croydon, CR0 4YY

To Patty, Shola, Maya, and Flo

Acknowledgements

I am deeply grateful to Ravi Kanbur, who initiated the Q-Squared initiative, and invited me to join on. The momentum in favour of mixed method analysis of poverty over the past decade has been highly influenced by Ravi's efforts. In the absence of such, this book would not exist.

I am also extremely appreciative of the support provided by the International Development Research Centre (IDRC), Canada. The IDRC financed a Q^2 research project which supported the organisation of conferences in Toronto and Hanoi, the development of a training programme, pilot studies and a Working Paper series (presently on-line at <www.trentu.ca/ids/qsquared.php>). Particular thanks go to Randy Spence for his continual encouragement, support, and wise advice.

The empirical chapters of this book benefitted greatly from the feedback of participants and discussants at a number of conferences and workshops over the years, including: the International Conference on Poverty and Inequality, United Nations Development Program and the World Bank Institute, Kuala Lumpur, Malaysia, 11–13 December 2007; Q-Squared in Policy: A Conference on Experiences of Combining Qualitative and Quantitative Methods in Decision-Making, Centre for Analysis and Forecasting, Vietnamese Academy of Social Sciences, Hanoi, 7–8 July 2007; the Chronic Poverty Research Centre (CPRC) Workshop on Integrating Panel Surveys and Life History Methods, London, Overseas Development Institute, 24–25 February 2006; the IDRC/ Poverty and Economic Policy (PEP) Program General Meeting, Colombo, Sri Lanka, 13–17 June 2005; Q-Squared in Practice: A Conference on Experiences of Combining Qualitative and Quantitative Methods in Poverty Appraisal. Centre for International Studies, University of Toronto, 15–16 May 2004; the Poverty Analysis and Data Initiative (PADI) Regional Workshop, World Bank, Mombasa, Kenya, 7–8 May 2004; the Roundtable Meeting on Encouraging Complementarities between Qualitative and Quantitative Poverty Appraisal, Cornell University/Institute of Statistical, Social and Economic Research (ISSER), University of Ghana, Accra. 21–22 May 2003; the UNDP Regional Workshop on Poverty Reduction, Kathmandu, Nepal, 2–4 October 2002; the Conference on Combining Qualitative and Quantitative Methods in Development Research, Centre for Development Studies, University of Wales Swansea. Swansea,

Wales, 1–2 July 2002 and the Workshop on Qualitative and Quantitative Poverty Appraisal: Complementarities, Tensions and the Way Forward, Cornell University, Ithaca, NY, 15–16 March 2001.

Some of the theoretical materials in Chapter 2 originally appeared in my unpublished DPhil thesis from the Institute of Development Studies, University of Sussex, entitled 'The Poverty Debate with application to the Republic of Guinea'. I am particularly grateful to my supervisors, Michael Lipton and Reginald Green, along with the Martin Greeley, William Outhwaite, Peter Penz, and Paul Seabright, whose comments on materials in this chapter led to significant improvements. Support from the Social Sciences and Humanities Research Council (SSHRC) of Canada, which facilitated completion of my thesis work, is gratefully acknowledged.

Most of this book was completed during a sabbatical from the Department of International Development Studies at Trent University, Canada. I am very fortunate to have excellent students and fantastic colleagues at Trent, on whom I've tried out some of the ideas in this book over the years. In particular, I'd like to thank Haroon Akram-Lodhi, Feyzi Baban, Dana Barker Gee, Chris Beyers, Winnie Lem, and Jackie Solway.

I am also very grateful to my editors at Oxford University Press for their support, patience and understanding. Particular thanks are due Aimee Wright and Adam Swallow.

My greatest debt is to my family, Patty, Shola, Maya, and Flo who put everything in perspective.

Contents

List of Figures

List of Tables

Part I
Introduction

Chapter 1

Q-Squared: Combining Qualitative and Quantitative Approaches to Poverty Analysis

The past decade or so has seen a vast quantity of analytical work under-taken on poverty in the Global South. International organizations and inter-national research consortia have generated a sizeable body of literature, synthesized in research reports such as the Chronic Poverty Research Centre's *Chronic Poverty Reports,* the International Fund of Agricultural Development's (IFAD) *Rural Poverty Reports*, and so forth. Further, there have been a series of 'best-seller' monographs, each with a different slant on core causes of, and remedies for, poverty. Examples include Jeffrey Sach's (2005) *The End of Poverty,* Paul Collier's (2007) *The Bottom Billion*, and Abhijit Banerjee and Ester Duflo's (2011) *Poor Economics*. There is no question that knowledge about poverty has flourished in recent years.

One is struck, however, by the nature of the evidentiary base used to sup-port core claims made in debates about poverty. Consider, for example, *The Bottom Billion* and *Poor Economics,* two of the most influential books on pov-erty to appear in recent years, replete with fascinating insights about the nature and causes of poverty. In the first case, there is a very heavy weight-ing on the results of econometric models to support key conclusions drawn. In the second case, findings from randomized controlled trials provide the core empirical support for claims made about poverty. Such methodological approaches are not 'good' or 'bad' in themselves, but they do have implica-tions for how we understand and explain poverty, and what we propose to do about it.

A core objective of this book is to examine the underlying assumptions and implications of how we conceptualize and investigate poverty. The empirical entry point for such inquiry is a series of research initiatives which have used mixed- method, or Q-squared (Q^2), approaches to poverty ana-lysis. Systematic review of the Q^2 literature is relevant in itself in that it high-lights the vast range of analytical tools within the social sciences which may be used to understand and explain social phenomena, along with interesting research results. This literature also serves as a lens to probe foundational concerns about knowledge claims made in poverty debates. Implicitly or explicitly, questions are raised about the reasons for emphasizing different dimensions of poverty and favouring different units of knowledge, the basis for distinguishing valid and invalid claims, the meaning of causation and nature of causal inference, and so forth. The burgeoning body of Q^2 literature, then, provides an entry point to address both foundational issues, about assumptions underlying approaches to poverty, and applied issues, about the strengths and limitations of different research methods and the ways they may be fruitfully combined.

The format of this chapter is as follows. Section 1.1 discusses the recent turn to mixed methods in the social sciences with emphasis on Q^2 traditions of poverty analysis. Definitional and conceptual issues are then reviewed in Sections 1.2, 1.3, and 1.4, which address the qualitative/quantitative distinction, types of mixed methods, and stages of poverty analysis, respectively. A final section lays out the objectives and format of the book.

1.1 Background: A Decade of Q^2

Mixed-method research in the social sciences has been on the ascendency over the past decade (Brannen 2005). A number of developments attest to this trend. New journals have emerged specializing in mixed-method analysis including the *Journal of Mixed Method Research* and the *International Journal of Multiple Research Approaches*. A second edition of the *SAGE Handbook of Mixed Methods in Social and Behavioral Research* was recently published after the first edition appeared in 2003 (Tashakkori and Teddle [2003] 2010). Annual conferences on mixed-method research have also been held for around eight years running (<http://www.healthcareconferences.leeds.ac.uk/conferences/>). In the ebb and flow of methodological fashion, mixed-method research is definitely in vogue.

The renewed focus on mixed-method inquiry has been equally evident in development studies, and, in particular, poverty analysis. While there is a long history of interdisciplinary research in development studies (Lipton 1970), the quantity and quality of such work has tended to be quite variable over time. The recent decade, however, has been marked by a significant increase in both the quantity and quality of materials produced.

There have been a number of initiatives to promote a more systematic integration of 'quantitative' and 'qualitative' approaches to poverty analysis in the Global South. Examples include research programmes or activities of the *BASIS Collaborative Research Support Program* formerly based at the University of Wisconsin-Madison and now at the University of California

Davis (<www.basis.ucdavis.edu), the *Chronic Poverty Research Centre* led by the University of Manchester and the Overseas Development Institute (<http://www.chronicpoverty.org/>), the *Global Poverty Research Group* at the Universities of Oxford and Manchester (<http://www.gprg.org/>), the International Food Policy Research Institute, in particular work conducted in East Africa, the *Livelihoods and Diversification Directions Explored by Research (LADDER)* research project at the University of East Anglia, the *Wellbeing Research in Developing Countries (WED)* project at the University of Bath (<http://www.welldev.org.uk/>), the World Bank, in particular their *Moving out of Poverty* studies, the *Young Lives* project led by the University of Oxford (<http://www.younglives.org.uk/>), and the *Stages of Progress approach* pioneered by Duke University's Anirudh Krishna and colleagues (<http://sanford.duke.edu/krishna/>), among others.

Another initiative in this same tradition was the Q^2 research programme led by Cornell University's Ravi Kanbur and the present author. Conferences were organized at Cornell University (2001), the University of Toronto (2004), and the Vietnamese Academy of Social Sciences (2007) dealing, respectively, with concepts and definitions, analysis, and policy. Results appeared in an edited monograph (Kanbur 2003) and special issues of *World Development* (Kanbur and Shaffer 2007a) and the *International Journal of Multiple Research Approaches* (Shaffer *et al.* 2008). With support from Canada's International Development Research Council (IDRC), the Q-Squared project developed a training programme and a website which housed the *Q-Squared Working Paper Series* (presently on-line at <www. trentu.ca/ids/qsquared.php>).

Much of the empirical work surveyed in Parts II and III of this book was completed in the context of one or more of these initiatives. There is no attempt to present an exhaustive survey of all Q^2-type work completed over the past decade. In general, studies have been selected which represent high-quality examples of ways of addressing specific issues which arise in poverty analysis.

More specifically, five main considerations guided the choice of materials covered. There is a focus on (i) the Global South; (ii) poverty; (iii) published sources; (iv) empirical findings; (v) results within the past decade. Accordingly, the following contributions, with relevance to Q^2, but not meeting the selection criteria, are not covered: (i) the large literatures on happiness (Layard 2005) and human well-being (McGillivray 2007); (ii) theoretical and methodological debates concerning the role of structure and agency and methodological individualism in poverty analysis (e.g. du Toit 2009; Harris 2009; da Corta 2011); (iii) analyses of theoretical underpinnings (Ruggeri Laderchi *et al.* 2003; Stewart *et al.* 2007) or conceptual foundations (Grusky and Kanbur 2006) of approaches to poverty; (iv) mixed-method studies dealing with related, but distinct, issues such as the Commons, or communally held land and natural resources (Kanbur and Riles 2006; Poteete *et al.* 2010), social capital (Grootaert and Narayan 2004), microfinance (Collins *et al.* 2009), HIV/AIDS (Seeley *et al.* 2008), and diverse issues in the 'new' economic sociology (Granovetter 2005).

1.2 The Qualitative/Quantitative Distinction

Many understand intuitively what is meant by the terms 'qualitative' and 'quantitative'. The former is often associated with 'words', the latter with 'numbers'. In the social sciences, the related distinction may be between disciplines such as social anthropology on the one hand, and economics or statistics on the other. Despite the intuitive sense of these terms, it is quite difficult to pin down a working definition of the qualitative/quantitative distinction that effectively distinguishes between approaches found in actual mixed-method designs. In fact, the qualitative/quantitative distinction has been interpreted in quite different ways over the years and has been the subject of some controversy (Bryman 1984).

To illustrate this point, it is useful to retrace the different interpretations given to these terms at the inaugural Q^2 conference at Cornell University in 2002, which focused on conceptual and definitional matters. There was wide-ranging debate among participants about what exactly the terms qualitative and quantitative were meant to signify. At least four different points of view were expressed.

Jesko Hentschel (1999, 2003) argued that the relevant distinction was between types of data, qualitative and quantitative, and types of data collection methods, 'more or less' contextual. Contextual methods are those which attempt to understand social phenomena in the context of their social, cultural, economic, and political environment. Another set of categories was provided by Chris Barrett (2003), who distinguished between specific to general research on the one hand, and subject or researcher-driven research on the other. This latter distinction is close to that of Robert Chambers (2003a), who distinguished between participatory and 'established' approaches. Another axis of differentiation advanced by Erik Thorbecke (2003) and Luc Christiaensen (2003) was between deductive and inductive inferential processes.

In his attempt to synthesize these diverse positions, Ravi Kanbur (2003) proposed a typology of difference based on five elements: (i) type of information on population (non-numerical or numerical); (ii) type of population coverage (specific to general); (iii) type of population involvement (active to passive); (iv) type of inference methodology (inductive to deductive); (v) type of disciplinary framework (broad social sciences to neoclassical economics). This typology serves the useful purpose of unpacking the 'qual/quant' terminology by highlighting exactly what is being mixed. Arguably, however, these distinctions are hard to sustain in light of empirical counterexamples (Shaffer 2005; Kanbur and Shaffer 2007b). A few examples illustrate this point.

The numerical/non-numerical distinction poses problems because it is possible to numerically transform almost any type of information by counting, scaling, ranking, and so forth. Such transformation may take place at the point of data collection or analysis. Many examples are presented in Parts II and III of this book. The distinction does have some cutting power in that the process of numerical transformation is different for different types of information, based on how closely they map onto an existing scale (Shaffer 2005; Kanbur and Shaffer 2007b). For example, data on food consumption are defined in terms of either quantities consumed or the expenditure required to purchase them. Nevertheless, the numerical/non-numerical distinction is ambiguous as phrased and needs further unravelling.

A second distinction, between specific and general population coverage, is arguably more *incidental* than *essential* to the 'qualitative/quantitative' divide. Just about any research technique, qualitative or quantitative, may be conducted in few or many sites. Fixed-response questionnaires may be applied in a single site such as Shaffer's (1998) study of gender and poverty in the Republic of Guinea discussed in Chapter 3. Likewise, some participatory poverty assessments have national coverage, such as that of Rwanda discussed in Chapter 4 (Howe and McKay 2007). Further, the content of fixed response household surveys and focus group or interview guides may be modified to be more or less context specific. This issue of population coverage probably depends on (i) the purpose of the research, in particular whether results are required to be representative of a broader population, say to inform decision making at regional or national levels; (ii) the nature of the extrapolation exercise, specifically whether statistical inference is being used to extrapolate results, which implies some type of probabilistic sampling and a minimum sample size; (iii) practical considerations related to cost and standardization, which tend to favour fixed-response questionnaires for studies with more observations. As above, the distinction based on population coverage is hard to sustain.

A final distinction between neoclassical economics and other disciplines understates important 'quantitative' traditions within the social sciences. There are arguably greater affinities than differences of method between neoclassical economists and rational choice political scientists, sociologists schooled in the Lazarsfeld tradition of surveying and model building, 'cliometric' historians, and so on (Abbott 2001). As with the other distinctions, it is likely that the disciplinary distinction requires further refinement.

Most such attempts at taxonomy lead to an impasse from which there are two recourses. The first is to 'go foundational', and search for more basic categories from which the intermediate categories in typologies such as Kanbur's derive. An attempt is made to do this in Chapter 2, which examines epistemological underpinnings of approaches to poverty. The second recourse is to eschew typologies and describe what exactly is being combined in specific cases. We opt for this latter path throughout the empirical chapters in Parts II and III when individual studies are examined. Accordingly, throughout this book, the qualitative/quantitative terminology is largely eschewed in favour of discussion of the actual methods or data that are being mixed.

1.3 Types of Mixed Methods

As with the qualitative/quantitative distinction, there have been a large number of typologies of mixed-method research designs. Such frameworks perform the useful function of outlining different ways of combining research methods and the diverse purposes such mixing may serve. Further, some distinctions in the typologies are revisited in Chapter 8, which summarizes key arguments, and in Appendix A, which presents a quick reference guide to the approaches to poverty discussed throughout the book.

An influential early typology, developed by Jennifer Greene and colleagues (1989), placed emphasis on five core purposes of mixed-method research, namely triangulation, complementarity, development, initiation, and expansion. In its original definition, triangulation was meant to denote the use of a range of methods with known off-setting biases (Mathison 1988). The intent is to enhance validity if research results are broadly convergent using different methods. Complementarity, on the other hand, uses multiple methods to investigate different but overlapping issues with a view to clarify, elaborate upon, or better interpret the results of one method with those from another. Development refers to the use of methods from one approach to assist in the methodological development of another through, say, using focus groups to better structure the wording of fixed response surveys. In the case of initiation, the aim is to use contradictory or paradoxical results generated by different research approaches to initiate further inquiry as to the reasons why. Finally, expansion refers to the use of different methods to address related, but distinct, components in an overall research question. A frequent example in the mixed-method literature, illustrated in Chapters 6 and 7, is the use of mixed methods to combine analysis of outcomes and processes or results and mechanisms.

Another typology is based on the work of Janice Morse (1991, 2003), who developed a widely used notational system for categorizing mixed-methods designs. Morse's schema distinguished between simultaneous and sequential forms of mixing along with designs which afforded priority to one method over the other. In terms of notation, the plus sign (+) is used to denote simultaneity while arrows (→) are used to indicate sequencing. Priority is reflected in the use of upper or lower case for qualitative and quantitative designs. So, for example, a research design which begins with a small focus group to develop a large, core fixed-response household survey which is subsequently followed up with additional focus groups to explain results would be represented as: qual→QUAN→qual.

There are many additional categorical schemes, some of which combine elements of the above two typologies (Creswell *et al.* 2003). Others introduce new elements such as the stages in the research process at which mixing occurs and the nature of the inferential process (Tashakkori and Teddle 2003b). A good review of such schemes is presented in Abbas Tashakkori and Charles Teddle's (2003a) introductory chapter to the *Handbook of Mixed Methods*.

Typologies of mixed method designs are useful for certain purposes such as clarification of research methodology and objectives. They may also serve as an organizing framework for the discussion of specific mixed-method studies. In Parts II and III of this book, however, we refrain from using such typologies and refer to exactly how mixing occurs in particular studies. The organizing framework for the empirical studies reviewed is based on specific issues and challenges found within the identification and causal stages of poverty analysis, defined in the following section.

A final point concerns the terminology of 'disciplinarity', in particular the distinction between cross-, multi-, and interdisciplinarity. As with the qualitative/quantitative distinction, a number of definitions appear in the literature. Ravi Kanbur (2002), for example, proposed one set of distinctions based on the degree of integration across disciplines. In this formulation, cross-disciplinarity refers to analysis or policy recommendations based substantively on the methods and analytical techniques of more than one discipline. Multidisciplinarity occurs when researchers from different disciplines work independently using their own methods and analytical approaches and subsequently synthesize results bearing on a common or related question. Finally, interdisciplinarity is defined as 'deep integration, right from the beginning...an inextricable interweaving of the different disciplinary approaches' (Kanbur 2002: 483).

Throughout this book, we will not maintain distinctions of this sort. The term interdisciplinary will be used as shorthand for mixed methods which could conceivably fall within any of Kanbur's three categories of 'disciplinarity'.

1.4 Stages of Poverty Analysis

The main organizing framework for this book is based on two stages of poverty analysis. The first stage, identification, asks 'who are the poor' and 'what are their characteristics'. The second stage, causal analysis, asks 'why are they poor'. Part II of this book is about identification while Part III is about causal analysis.

Many additional questions and issues arise within both of these stages of poverty analysis. In the identification stage, it is necessary to decide upon the dimensions of poverty to include and exclude, the weights to assign these dimensions if more than one is selected, the level at which to set a poverty line, the ways to aggregate or count those who fall below the threshold, and so forth. Challenges also arise for interpersonal comparisons of well-being when different dimensions of poverty (the 'basket' problem) or different reference levels of achievement (the 'levels' problem) are selected by different populations. Such issues form the basis of the organizing framework presented in Section 4.1, within which the individual studies are situated.

Within the causal stage of poverty analysis, a wide range of issues arise. A preliminary distinction is between causal analysis of poverty status at one or more points of time and of poverty dynamics or the flow of households into and out of poverty. In addition, challenges arise with respect to the causal framework, in particular finding ways to improve upon causal variables, weights, mechanisms, and the causal 'tree.' Such challenges form the basis of the organizing framework used to categorize the empirical studies, presented in Section 6.1.

1.5 Objectives and Format

The aim of this book is twofold. First, a core objective is to make explicit foundational assumptions which underlie different ways of understanding and explaining poverty and to show how they matter. It is argued that such assumptions have implications for the analytical categories and tools we use in poverty analysis, and for research results. The emphasis on foundations serves as a riposte to many poverty debates which have been cast in excessively technical terms. There has been far too much discussion of method and insufficient attention to such issues as what counts as reliable knowledge and 'hard' evidence, how to ascertain validity, how causation is defined and causal claims established empirically, and so forth. This point is important because some strong claims are found in the literature about the nature of poverty which rest on equally strong, but hidden, foundational assumptions about the analytical approach adopted.

The second objective is to conduct a critical review of the vast range of applied tools of poverty analysis and show how they may be fruitfully combined. Poverty analysis has been a growth industry over the past twenty years or so, and the range of methods on display has grown accordingly. Q^2 type studies have shown a high degree of methodological innovation, making use of varied information types, data collection techniques, and forms of analysis. It is useful for both academic and applied purposes to critically assess this body of literature paying due regards to its merits and demerits.

The format of the book is as follows. Part II is concerned with identification issues, specifically the meanings and dimensions of poverty. Chapter 2 begins with a discussion of epistemological foundations of the consumption and dialogical approaches to poverty analysis with emphasis on contrasting units of knowledge and validity criteria. Chapter 3 proceeds to investigate if these two approaches identify different population groups as 'poor', drawing on results of 'first generation' Q^2 studies. Subsequent methodological developments within the 'second generation' Q^2 tradition are then explored in Chapter 4 focusing on ways to enhance comparability and validity of results across diverse populations.

Part III addresses causal analysis. Chapter 5 explores foundational issues concerning conceptions of causation and models of causal inference. Chapter 6 explores certain of the methodological implications for Q^2 approaches to causal analysis of poverty status and poverty dynamics. Chapter 7 extends the discussion to Q^2 approaches to impact assessment. A common theme running through Chapters 6 and 7 is that Q^2 analyses can lead to a fuller understanding of causation by expanding upon, or improving, aspects of the causal framework used in poverty analysis.

A quick reference guide to the Q^2 studies discussed in the book is presented in Appendix A based on a modified version of some of the typologies of mixed method designs presented in Section 1.3.

Part II
Identification: Who are the Poor and What are Their Characteristics?

Chapter 2

Foundations: Epistemology[1]

> World languages compete with each other for the number of words refer-
> ring to the stations and conditions associated with the different percep-
> tions of poverty. In Persian, there are more than thirty words for naming
> those who for one reason or another, are perceived as poor. In most
> African languages, at least three to five words have been identified for
> poverty. The Torah uses eight for the purposes. In the Middle Ages, the
> words covering the range of conditions under the concept are well over
> forty. (Rahnema 1991: 6)

What is meant by the word 'poverty'? The above quotation suggests that
poverty means different things to different people at different times, including to poverty analysts who make decisions about which dimensions of poverty to emphasize. But, why are some definitions chosen over others? What
is the basis for determining that poverty should focus, say, on low levels of
consumption expenditure rather than low levels of social status?

It is argued that part of the explanation for the choice of the definition of
poverty is due to often buried epistemological commitments made to broad
traditions of inquiry. Epistemology is the branch of philosophy which studies the nature and claims of knowledge. Issues of epistemology are quite
integral to many aspects of poverty analysis, though they are rarely made
explicit.

The view that 'epistemology matters' to poverty analysis is based on two
arguments. First, there are historical linkages between epistemological traditions and those bodies of theory which make up the consumption approach
to poverty. Epistemological considerations have explicitly guided the development of these theoretical perspectives. Second, in the case of dialogical
approaches, there is no such clear historical linkage, though there are quite
marked affinities with epistemological positions.

---

[1] Parts of this chapter draw on Shaffer (2002, 2005) and Kanbur and Shaffer (2007).

It must be recognized however, that epistemology is not the *only* thing that determines the choice of the definition of poverty in use. Other potential factors include political considerations, relating, say, to the imperative of providing certain types of evidence to sway public opinion, attitudinal inclinations concerning, say, the desire of engaging in participatory research, practical concerns related to cost and data quality, and so forth. The relevance of such considerations does not undermine the core argument that epistemology *also* matters.

The format of this chapter is as follows: Section 2.1 outlines key characteristics of the consumption and dialogical approaches to poverty while Section 2.2 presents core features of two traditions of inquiry with different epistemological foundations, Empiricism and hermeneutics or critical hermeneutics. Sections 2.3 and 2.4 discuss the core units of knowledge in Empiricism and hermeneutics, respectively, while Sections 2.5 and 2.6 examine validity criteria in Empiricism and critical hermeneutics, respectively. Section 2.7 concludes.

2.1 Two Approaches to Poverty

There are a wide range of methods of poverty analysis which can be combined in many different ways. A core axis of differentiation, however, is between what will be called 'consumption' and 'dialogical' approaches to poverty analysis. The former has roots in the applied tradition of micro-economics while the latter is associated with applied work in social anthropology and in the tradition of participatory rural appraisal.

The consumption approach comes in a variety of forms (Boltvinik 1998). The present discussion will focus on one variant in widespread use in the Global South by international organizations such as the World Bank (Ravallion 1994; Haughton and Khandker 2009). In this approach, poverty is defined as the non-fulfilment of basic preferences, represented by (low) levels of consumption expenditure. Basic preferences are defined in terms of minimal levels of caloric intake, supplemented by an allowance for basic non-food consumption. Information on consumption expenditure is gathered through fixed-response household surveys containing large consumption modules. Such data allow for the estimation of poverty lines and the calculation of various poverty measures, such as the poverty 'head count'.

There are intermediate bodies of theory which underpin the consumption approach, namely nutrition science and two variants of utility theory: revealed preference theory and money metric utility. Utility theory is responsible for the emphasis on consumer preferences. Such preferences are known by observing actual consumer behaviour, or through responses to consumption questions in household surveys (*revealed preference theory*). Consumption is represented in monetary terms as levels of consumption expenditure (*money metric utility*). Nutrition science accounts for the anchoring of the poverty cut-off in terms of caloric intake. All of these aspects of consumption poverty have close linkages to epistemology.

The dialogical approach to poverty analysis relies heavily on dialogic techniques, such as focus group discussions, semi-structured interviews, and so forth to come to an understanding of locally relevant meanings of poverty. A major part of the analytical work consists of delineating the multiple dimensions of poverty and understanding their interrelationships. One example is the participatory approach to poverty, which has drawn heavily on the seminal work of Robert Chambers (1983). Since the mid-nineties, a large number of 'participatory poverty assessments' have been undertaken in the Global South, including the World Bank's 1998 *Voices of the Poor* exercise, which involved over 20,000 persons in over 200 communities in 23 countries (Narayan *et al.* 2002). Some social anthropological approaches to poverty also exemplify this tradition of poverty analysis (Tucker *et al.* 2011). In both cases, analysis involves interpreting local understandings of the meaning of poverty as revealed through dialogue.

It should be noted that there are important differences between the applied tradition of social anthropology and participatory rural appraisal. For example, the former has emphasized the imperative of combining the observation of behaviour (the etic) along with the understanding of meanings (the emic) and analysing discrepancies between the two (Booth *et al.* 2006).[2] Further, ethnographic work tends to be of much longer duration involving more detailed inquiry and generating a more intimate knowledge of local conditions. Despite these differences, they both fall under the heading of 'dialogical poverty' in the emphasis placed on understanding local meanings of poverty using dialogical techniques.

2.2 Two Epistemological Traditions

Epistemology is about the sources and limitations of knowledge. It addresses such questions as 'what do we know' and 'how do we know what we know'? Answers to these questions distinguish different research traditions in the social sciences. A widely used typology differentiates between Empiricist, hermeneutic (interpretative) and critical hermeneutic traditions of inquiry

---

[2] This reliance on techniques of participant observation, and associated importance placed on intersubjective observability, is one reason that some of the founders of anthropology considered the new discipline to be empiricist in the sense discussed in Section 2.2 (Wright and Nelson 1995: 43–51).

(Fay 1975; Braybrooke 1987). It will be argued that there are important links between Empiricism and the consumption approach to poverty and between hermeneutics, or critical hermeneutics, and dialogical approaches.

There are a number of ways to distinguish these research traditions. Emphasis is here placed on the basic unit of knowledge which comprises them, along with the ways they ascertain the validity of knowledge claims. These two issues are also key distinguishing factors between the consumption and dialogical approaches to poverty.

In its most basic form, Empiricism maintains that our concepts and knowledge claims are based ultimately on experience or experiential knowledge. The idea has ancient roots (Lipton 2001), but was prominently argued in the seventeenth and eighteenth centuries by the British philosophers, John Locke, George Berkeley, and David Hume (Bennett 1971). In the twentieth century, Empiricism was modified in a variety of ways by the logical positivists in the 1920s and 1930s and subsequently by the logical empiricists and the philosopher Karl Popper (Caldwell 1982). Some of the differences between these traditions of thought are discussed in Section 2.5. Our major focus will be on those versions of Empiricism which have influenced utility theory, nutrition science, and consumption poverty.

Empiricism can be defined in terms of its basic unit of knowledge and validity criteria. In terms of the former, particular importance is placed on so-called 'brute data'. Such data play a critical role in the selection of conceptual categories, such as poverty, and in adjudicating knowledge claims. Empiricism assigns a special role to 'intersubjective observability' in determining the validity of knowledge claims. As discussed in Section 2.5, there is a close relationship between brute data and intersubjective observability.

Hermeneutics is the interpretive understanding of social phenomena. Like Empiricism, it has multiple and diverse roots dating from antiquity (Grodin 1994). In modern times, it has been associated with continental philosophers, such as Martin Heidegger and Hans-Georg Gadamer, the *verstehen* tradition of sociology of Wilhelm Dilthey and Max Weber, along with the later work of Cambridge philosopher Ludwig Wittgenstein, in particular his emphasis on 'language games' and forms of life, as interpreted by Peter Winch (Bernstein 1976). The critical hermeneutic tradition is foremost associated with the work of the German social theorist Jürgen Habermas.

In contrast to Empiricism, the core units of knowledge in hermeneutic inquiry are so-called 'intersubjective meanings'. Such information are essential to understand or 'make sense' of social phenomena. In terms of ascertaining validity, a discourse-based approach is favoured rather than one based on observability. Critical hermeneutics, as here defined, differs from hermeneutics in that it demands critical assessment of given points of view and not simply their interpretation.

The remainder of this chapter further explores epistemological differences between Empiricism and critical hermeneutics concerning units of knowledge and validity criteria. The objective is to link such differences to the consumption and dialogical approaches to poverty in order to show how 'epistemology matters'.

2.3 Empiricism and Knowledge

We have already commented on the central role that brute data have played in Empiricism and the consumption approach to poverty as the bedrock of knowledge and arbiter of validity claims. The term 'brute data' is being used in the sense of philosopher Charles Taylor (1985: 19) as 'data whose validity cannot be questioned by offering another interpretation or reading'. But what exactly are the characteristics of these types of data and why are they so important to consumption poverty? To address these questions, it is necessary first to present a brief history of the relationship between brute data and Empiricism and then to link it to utility theory, nutrition science, and consumption poverty.

The early Empiricists originally conceived of brute data as sense data, 'the things that are immediately known in sensation: such things as colours, sounds, smells, hardnesses, roughnesses, and so on' (Russell 1952: 12). They provided the basis of a phenomenalist theory of knowledge, the view that the 'indubitable objects of knowledge are the immediate "impressions" or "sense contents" of...sensory experience' (Nagel 1961: 120). Alternatively, this view has been labelled the 'copy principle', that our concepts are images or copies of the sensory impressions which precede them (Lipton 2001).

Sense data began to lose their central importance in Empiricist circles following their rejection by Karl Popper and some of the twentieth-century logical positivists, primarily Otto Neurath and Rudolf Carnap (Ayer 1959: 17–21). Three key considerations contributed to their downfall. First, it was increasingly acknowledged that that sense data were not infallible as claimed (Ayer 1959: 20). Second, there was growing rejection of the view that all concepts could be translated into actual or possible sensations (Nagel 1961: 121–125). Third, and most important, it was increasingly recognized that *private* sensations could not serve as the basis of *public*, intersubjective knowledge claims (Putnam 1981: 181). As a result, sense data were superseded by physical data with intersubjectively observable properties.

Intersubjective observability is critical in that it addresses the last objection to sense data by allegedly establishing the subject-invariance of properties of objects.[3] Harré (1985: 159) paraphrases this requirement: 'many qualities [of objects] vary with the state of the subject, the perceiver, while for scientific purposes we should choose those qualities which are subject invariant'. In this revised sense then, brute data are physical, intersubjectively observable and subject-invariant. The classic statement of the new conception of brute data is provided by Popper (1959: 103) in his discussion of 'basic statements': '...a basic statement must also satisfy a material requirement...this event must be an *"observable"* event; that is to say, basic statements must be testable, inter-subjectively, by "observation"'.

What are the implications for consumption poverty? To recall, two versions of utility theory, revealed preference theory and money metric utility, along with nutrition science are the theoretical foundations of the consumption approach to poverty. Both have been influenced by Empiricism's preoccupation with brute data.

Utility theory is the successor to the philosophic tradition of Utilitarianism. David Hume may be considered as the intellectual source of this doctrine (Plamenatz 1958: 22) in his attempt to derive the object of moral value (virtue) from sensory experience. In his discussion of virtue and vice, Hume (1988: 468–9) writes: '...see if you can find the matter of fact or real existence which you call *vice*...you will never find it till you turn your reflexion into your own breast, and find a sentiment of disapprobation, which arises in you towards this action. Here is a matter of fact'. The centrality of empirical fact in Hume's moral theory is a function of his Empiricism. He hoped to explain moral terms without recourse to non-empirical entities using the 'experimental method':[4]

> The only object of [ethical] reasoning is to...observe that particular in which the estimable qualities agree on the one hand, and the blameable on the other; and thence to reach the foundation of ethics...It is full time...[to] reject every system of ethics, however subtle or ingenious, which is not founded on fact and observation Hume. (1902: 174–175)

Jeremy Bentham, probably the most famous proponent of Utilitarianism, was deeply influenced by Hume (Baumgardt 1966) and followed him in grounding the object of value, the principle of utility or the greatest happiness principle, in the human sentiment of happiness. Bentham (1948: 18) favoured this principle over other evaluative standards because it 'is clearer, as referring more explicitly to pain and pleasure'. Further, he maintained that pleasure and pain are directly measurable so that evaluative judgments could be made

---

[3] Observations statements are themselves fallible, a point which is widely recognized today (Chalmers 1999).

[4] Hume's experiments were really thought exercises, immune from empirical refutation (Noxon 1973: 116–123).

according to an intersubjectively observable 'felicific calculus' (Bentham 1948: 29). Bentham's Utilitarianism was incorporated in utility theory by one of the founders of neo-classical economics, Stanley Jevons, who explicitly credited Bentham as the source of his ideas (Howey 1989), and argued forcefully that 'the object of Economy is to maximize happiness by purchasing pleasure, as it were, at the lowest cost of pain' (Jevons 1871: vii–viii).

In modern utility theory, the object of value has become the physical state of preference fulfilment rather than happiness or pleasure. Nobel laureate in economics Paul Samuelson is a central figure. He developed revealed preference theory (Samuelson 1966) and was an enthusiastic proponent of money metric utility. According to Samuelson (1974: 1262), money metric utility is 'objectively measurable' and 'defined behavioristically', without the need for 'psychological introspection' by virtue of revealed preference theory. Revealed preference theory was an attempt to base consumer theory on intersubjectively observable information, an orientation 'more directly based upon those elements which must be taken as *data* by economic science' (Samuelson 1966: 13). Revealed preference theory rendered preferences intersubjectively observable and money metric utility *allegedly* restored interpersonal comparability to utility following its earlier rejection as unscientific (Robbins 1962: 138–139).

Nutrition science is the second theoretical underpinning of the consumption approach to poverty. It allows for the determination of the caloric content of different foodstuffs and the calculation of minimal caloric requirements of categories of persons (Taylor and Pye 1966). The former is measured by heat released when proteins, fats, and carbohydrates are burned in bomb or oxycalorimeters and represented as a heat unit, a calorie. The latter can be measured on the basis of carbon dioxide excreted at rest, the basal metabolic rate (BMR), and during different types of physical activity using a respiration calorimeter.[5] Human energy requirements can be calculated for distinct population subgroups based on such factors affecting the BMR such as body size, shape, and composition as well as on different activity levels. In both of these cases, inquiry proceeds on the basis of controlled experimentation with intersubjectively observable, physical data as the key informational source.[6]

The incorporation of nutrition science into the modern analysis of consumption poverty is often retraced to the poverty studies undertaken by Seebohm Rowntree (1980) in 1899 in York, England (Townsend 1979: 33–34,

---

[5] In practice, measurement is complicated, *inter alia*, by biological and behavioural adaptation to nutrition stress which reduce dietary energy requirements (Osmani 1992; Payne and Lipton 1994).

[6] There are important differences, and potential tensions, between the reliance on brute data in the context of casual observation and in controlled experiments, (MacIntyre 2007: 80–81), though the centrality of brute data as the core referent for adjudication remains.

Sen 1981: 11). In order to calculate minimal food costs associated with his concept of 'primary poverty', Rowntree relied upon estimates derived by the nutritionist Wilbur Atwater of minimal caloric requirements of male adult equivalents as well as the caloric value of different foodstuffs. Atwater, 'the father of American nutrition' established the blueprint which guided much subsequent nutrition research (McCollum 1957; Taylor and Pye 1966). While part of Rowntree's motivation was political, to sway public opinion with 'hard' evidence (Rowntree 1941), it is clear that Rowntree, a chemist by training, placed great stock on nutrition science as a means of rigorously establishing the primary poverty cut-off and expressly sought to inject added rigour to the measurement of poverty (Drinkwater 1960; Briggs 1961).

Following Rowntree, the poverty line in many variants of consumption poverty has been anchored on caloric intake using the techniques of nutrition science. While this preoccupation may find justification on practical or normative grounds, importance has been placed on the epistemological and methodological considerations. Allegedly, a nutrition-based requirement represents a basic human need whose adequacy level can be estimated in an 'objective' way. For example, a pioneer in poverty measurement using this approach, Molly Orshansky (1965: 5), explained her decision to anchor human need on dietary energy adequacy as follows: 'there is no generally acceptable standard for adequacy of essentials of living except food'.[7] Michael Lipton (1983: 6), another important figure in poverty analysis, proposes a nutrition-based definition on grounds that, *inter alia*, it possesses 'a definable "adequate level"'.

In summary, brute data are integral to the consumption poverty approach in three ways. First, levels of well-being, or preference fulfilment, are known through observation of consumer behaviour (revealed preference theory). Second, interpersonal comparisons of well-being can allegedly be made in intersubjectively observable fashion (money metric utility). Third, the estimation of the poverty line can be conducted on the basis of intersubjectively observable data (nutrition science). Brute data comprise the key unit of knowledge making up the consumption approach to poverty.

2.4 Hermeneutics and Knowledge

In the hermeneutic and critical hermeneutic traditions, the core unit of knowledge shifts from brute data to intersubjective meanings. The latter can be defined as the core categories, beliefs, and values which give sense to

---

[7] Political considerations were also quite integral to Orshansky's choice of methods (Fisher 1992).

social phenomena and meaning to social action. Putnam (1981: 201–202) provides a good example:

> Take the sentence 'the cat is on the mat'. We have the category 'cat' because we regard the division of the world into *animals* and *non-animals* as significant, and we are further interested in what *species* a given animal belongs to...We have the category 'mat' because we regard the division of inanimate things into *artifacts* and non-*artifacts* as significant, and we are further interested in the *purpose* and *nature* a particular artifact has...We have the category 'on' because we are interested in *spatial relations*...Notice what we have: we took the most banal statement imaginable, 'the cat' is on the mat', and we found that the presuppositions which make this statement a relevant [or meaningful] one in certain contexts include the significance of the categories *animate/inanimate, purpose* and *space.*

The concept of intersubjective meanings is central to the fundamental claim of hermeneutics and critical hermeneutics that social phenomena are 'intrinsically meaningful'. That is, social phenomena depend for their existence, and/or significance, on the meanings ascribed to them by social actors. Phenomena such as poverty are constituted, in part, by the intersubjective meanings given to them and interpreted by social actors, including researchers. If these claims are accepted, it follows that explaining social phenomena requires an understanding of intersubjective meanings. Failure to do so may seriously bias analysis: 'we interpret all other societies in the categories of our own' (Taylor 1985: 42).

A number of important methodological implications become apparent when examining how hermeneutics differs from Empiricism with respect to the so-called subject/object distinction (Sayer 1984). Brute data allows for the distinction between the subject and object of inquiry in that the latter, allegedly, is not open to multiple interpretations due to its intersubjectively observable characteristics. The distinction is *ontologically* trivial in that there is always someone conducting the inquiry (a subject) who may be distinguished from whatever he or she is inquiring about (the object). It is *epistemologically* significant, however, in that it demands that the characteristics of the object of inquiry not depend essentially on whoever happens to be conducting the scientific exercise.

In the consumption approach to poverty, the subject/object distinction guides data collection through fixed-response household surveys in that interaction between interviewer and respondent is carefully controlled and structured. A good statement is found in a guide to the World Bank's Living Standards Measurement Surveys (Grosh and Glewwe 1995: 6):

> Several features of the questionnaire help to minimize interviewer error... requiring virtually no decision-making by the interviewer. All of the questions

are written out exactly as they are to be asked.... these features reduce the conceptual skills required of the interviewers and the potential for variation among them.

The hermeneutic and critical hermeneutic traditions, by contrast, reject the subject/object distinction even as an idealized depiction of social inquiry. Understanding intersubjective meanings requires participation in a dialogic process whereby the subject and object of inquiry are interdependent. According to this view, the inquiring subject necessarily affects the object of his/her inquiry.

In the social sciences, the object of inquiry consists of a social world which is pre-interpreted by social actors. The task is to interpret *existing* interpretations, a process which has been labelled the 'double hermeneutic' (Giddens 1976: 162). For the hermeneutic tradition, accessing this pre-interpreted world 'fundamentally requires participation in a process of reaching understanding' (Habermas 1984: 112). Participation is essential because there is no other way to come to an understanding of intersubjective meanings. Interpreting individual responses to say, attitudinal questionnaire surveys, without a prior understanding of their intersubjective referents simply imposes our conceptual categories on everyone else (Sayer 1984: 33–35).

Participation entails the rejection of a *categorical* subject/object distinction because it is neither possible nor desirable to remove the effect of the investigator. 'Subjects' and 'objects' are intertwined in an intersubjective process consisting of participants in dialogue (Habermas 1991: 26).

This reciprocal relationship between subjects and objects in the process of understanding is known as reflexivity. In Empiricist circles, reflexivity is considered a *potential problem* due to the 'investigator effect'. It calls for practical solutions in terms of greater standardization of research design to minimize bias (Marsh 1979: 301–302). In the hermeneutic tradition, reflexivity is a *necessary feature* of social scientific inquiry premised on an interactive model of understanding. There are important implications for validity criteria, discussed in Sections 2.5 and 2.6.

Intersubjective meanings lie at the heart of the dialogical approach to poverty. A core objective is to better understand what is meant by poverty, what categories are considered relevant when thinking about well-being, what types of social relationships are important when analysing social change, and so forth. Inquiry of this sort involves dialogic processes such as focus groups and semi-structured interviews. While the dialogical approach is not *only* about intersubjective meanings, it is nevertheless predicated on an understanding of such, which constitutes the foundation of all subsequent analysis.

2.5 Empiricism and Validity

A second difference between Empiricism and hermeneutics concerns validity criteria. Empiricism relies on an observation-based model to establish the truth or validity of statements in which brute data play a special role. The nature of this role has changed over time but the centrality of brute data to validity determination has persisted.

For many of the early Empiricists, brute data represented an external reality, whether ideal or real. Many held a metaphysical conception of truth, closely tied to questions about the nature of 'reality'. Central to his conception of truth was a 'similitude' theory of reference which holds that there is a literal similarity between representations in our minds (of brute data) and the external objects to which they refer. The immediacy of sense data is the guarantor of this similarity (Putnam 1981: 57).

The rejection of metaphysics as 'meaningless' by the logical positivists lead to a shift in emphasis to the non-metaphysical truth, or validity, of statements (Ayer 1959: 116, 118–119). The effect was to closely link truth/validity criteria to intersubjectively observability. Truth no longer relied on a mysterious relation of correspondence to an external reality, nor on a subjective sense of certainty about the validity of immediate sense impressions. It was founded on the intersubjectively observable and subject-invariant properties of brute data themselves: 'Since the properties ascribed to things are observable properties, physicalist language thus is intersubjective, and there is no problem in determining the truth [validity] of assertions in physicalist language—one merely observes and sees whether the thing has the claimed property' (Suppes 1974: 13).

Accordingly, determination of the validity of theoretical statements became a process of establishing their correspondence to intersubjectively observable, subject-invariant, physical data. The particular correspondence criteria or rules of choice have been the subject of considerable debate over the years (Caldwell 1984). Proposals include strict verifiability of logical positivists, whereby all theoretical terms had to be defined in terms of an observation vocabulary and individual tested, confirmability of the logical empiricists, which allows for partial definition of theoretical terms and testing of theoretical systems as a whole, and falsifiability of philosopher Karl Popper, whereby the derivative hypothesizes of theories are subject to critical tests set up to falsify them. While these correspondence criteria differ in important respects, they all converge in that brute data are the referents to which testing is applied.

Brute data have played a critical role in establishing validity in the consumption poverty approach. At the level of data collection, consumption expenditure and actual food consumption can, in principle, be observed and questionnaire responses checked for forms of reporting biases (Scott and Amenuvegbe 1990; Jolliffe 2001). At the level of analysis, data on consumption expenditure and the poverty line determination may be reviewed and reanalysed to assess, say, the validity of empirical statements about poverty levels and trends. In addition, the validity of claims about, say, the causal importance of different variables may be tested econometrically as discussed in Chapter 6.

2.6 Critical Hermeneutics and Validity

The critical hermeneutic tradition generally rejects this central role of inter-subjective observability in establishing validity. The main reason is that narrative information generated by dialogic processes plays a much more central role in the analysis. There are a number of attempts to formulate truth or validity criteria within critical hermeneutics in ways which do not rely on the intersubjective observability requirement. One version, propounded by Jürgen Habermas, relies on a consensus theory of truth that rests on the premise that truth is the property of a statement which has been argumentatively, or discursively, validated (Habermas 1991).

The consensus theory of truth requires support from a number of theoretical concepts.[8] The most important is the ideal speech situation that serves, *inter alia*, as a means of distinguishing between true and false outcomes which are generated in discourse. It represents the idealized conditions which guarantee that a discursive consensus results only from the force of the better argument. It entails the absence of external constraints (force, threats) and internal constraints (ideology) on communicative action which requires 'a symmetrical distribution of chances to choose and to apply speech-acts' (Habermas 1991). Symmetry means equality in the opportunity to assume dialogue roles in different modes of speech.

The ideal speech situation serves, in part, as a regulative ideal or standard against which the validity of discursive outcomes may be assessed (Forester 1985). Although it may never be achieved, it may be approximated to differing degrees. This notion of an ideal speech situation has parallels with techniques used in some forms of participatory research, including certain participatory poverty assessments (PPAs), when dealing with issues of power (Drinkwater 1992).

Organizationally, the recognition of power impels greater attention to those either physically excluded from research encounters or present but unwilling or unable to participate. Various techniques have been developed

---

[8] A good discussion is found in Rehg (1994).

to facilitate wider participation including better identification of 'invisible' groups, organization of separate and/or smaller discussions for marginalized groups, organization of role plays where social roles are exchanged in order to subtly broach issues of power, and so on (Brock and McGee 2002). Together, these efforts at promoting more wide-ranging participatory dialogue may be construed, in part, as practical measures to better approximate the conditions of an ideal speech situation.

It is important not to overstate the effect of such measures in facilitating genuine participatory dialogue. A fundamental reason is the under-theorization of core concepts such as power and just deliberative outcomes (Kapoor 2002). It is for this reason that PPAs have co-existed happily with both the World Bank and organizations committed to much more transformative social change. It is certainly true that the 'critical' turn in PRA is limited and rests primarily at the procedural level. Nevertheless, the key point is that the basis of validity criteria shifts from the requirements of intersubjective observability to characteristics of dialogic inquiry.

2.7 Conclusion

Why then, does poverty mean inadequate basic preference fulfilment in the consumption approach to poverty and is left to be dialogically determined in the dialogical approach? Part of the explanation is epistemological.

For the consumption approach, the unit of knowledge and validity criteria in Empiricism figured prominently in utility theory and nutrition science. Specifically, utilitarianism and utility theory made the object of value, happiness, and subsequently preference fulfilment, a brute datum known without recourse to non-empirical entities. Further, levels of preference fulfilment became intersubjectively observable, through revealed preference theory, and amenable to interpersonal comparison, through money metric utility. Nutrition science allowed for the estimation of adequacy levels of caloric intake though controlled experiments based on brute data. The result is the conception of consumption poverty, anchored on inadequate caloric intake and measured by low levels of consumption expenditure. In this tradition of inquiry, determining the validity of statements about consumption poverty hinges on the intersubjectively observable nature of poverty data.

There are no such intermediate bodies of theory underlying the dialogical approach to poverty. Nevertheless, there are important similarities between its conceptualization of poverty and that of hermeneutics and critical hermeneutics. Intersubjective meanings substitute for brute data as the core unit of knowledge, while a discourse-based model of validity based on the characteristics of actual dialogue, substitutes for an observation-based model. As a consequence, the dialogical approach places emphasis on understanding diverse and local meanings of poverty and in creating conditions to facilitate more genuine, participatory dialogue.

Epistemology is deeply relevant to poverty analysis because it bears on the types of knowledge which are favoured and the types of validity criteria adopted. But does it matter in practice? Do different approaches identify different populations as poor? These questions are the subject of Chapter 3.

Chapter 3

First-Generation Q²: Exploring Differences

It was argued in Chapter 2 that epistemological differences matter for poverty analysis in that they account for different features of the consumption and dialogical approaches to poverty. Do such differences also matter for research outcomes? Do the consumption and dialogical approaches identify the same households, or households with the same characteristics, as poor? Do they come to the same conclusions about levels and trends of poverty?

The aim of this chapter is to shed light on these questions. The format is as follows. First, tools and methods used by the two approaches to poverty are summarized in Section 3.1. Section 3.2 reviews the results of empirical studies which have examined whether consumption and dialogical approaches to poverty generate conflicting research results. Section 3.3 offers potential explanations for the divergent results which the poverty approaches may generate, or the so-called 'micro–macro paradox'. Concluding remarks are presented in Section 3.4.

3.1 Consumption and Dialogical Approaches to Poverty: Tools and Methods

The consumption and dialogical approaches to poverty were introduced in Section 2.1, with a focus on their theoretical and conceptual underpinnings. This section discusses the tools and methods used by the two approaches to identify the poor and their characteristics, and to estimate levels and trends of poverty. It serves as background for Section 3.2 and Chapter 4, which review empirical results generated by the methods in question.

3.1.1 *The Consumption Approach*

There are four key issues which arise in identification stage of poverty analysis which serve as good entry points to review tools and methods. The first involves site selection, or sampling, and attendant claims about the 'representativeness' of data. The second concerns the chosen well-being metric, consumption expenditure, and associated issues of interpersonal comparisons. A third issue focuses on ways of drawing the poverty line. The final issue, aggregation, concerns measures or indices of poverty, and addresses the question of how to 'add-up' those who fall below the poverty line.

Often, the consumption approach aims to provide data which is nationally or regionally representative. To achieve this end, a sample of households is drawn from the total population, known, or estimated, from a recent population census. There are many issues in sampling and a wide range of sampling strategies (UNDESA 2005). A common theme, however, is that the probability that any household will be selected into the sample is known. It is on the basis of this probabilistic sampling that sample results are adjusted to reflect estimated values for the total population. In addition, probabilistic sampling allows for the calculation of standard errors and confidence intervals. Standard errors, which are calculated based on the variance and population size of the sample, provide an estimate of how far sample statistics differ from their 'true' values in the total population. Confidence intervals, calculated on the basis of standard errors, provide a range of plausible values for the unknown population parameters. In summary, probabilistic sampling and standard error estimation form the basis of claims that data on consumption poverty are representative of a broader population.

In terms of the well-being metric, the consumption approach is based on the total value of household consumption expenditure (Deaton and Grosh 2000). Consumption is generally preferred to income because it is measured with less error and is a better gauge of well-being over time as households can 'smooth' consumption by borrowing or drawing down on savings. Data on consumption expenditure are collected from large consumption modules in household surveys which ask respondents about the cost and/or quantities or various items consumed. A value is imputed for domestic consumption of own-produced goods, such as food, and for rent. In order to make consumption expenditure comparable across households, adjustments are made for different household composition, economies of scale in consumption[1] and price differences across sites or over time. Other adjustments are required such as assigning missing values to observations, adjusting for outliers in the data and so forth. At the end of this process, the consumption aggregate is derived which serves as the core well-being indicator or metric.

Once the consumption aggregate is calculated the next step is to draw a poverty line, allowing for the distinction between the poor and non-poor.

---

[1] Household economies of scale in consumption account for the fact that it is often cheaper for a larger family to consume goods because of fixed costs, bulk purchasing, and so on.

There are a wide range of conceptual approaches to setting a poverty line and methods for doing so (Boltvinik 1998). This discussion is limited to one of two nutrition-based approaches,[2] the food-share method, which is in widespread use in the Global South by national statistical agencies and international organization such as the World Bank. The food share method follows a five-step procedure to calculate a basic food poverty line (Haughton and Khandker 2009):

1. First, a 'poor' reference group is selected, which may be the bottom 20% or 30% of the consumption distribution.

2. Second, the caloric intake of the reference group is calculated based on the quantity of food items consumed, and the caloric content of these items.

3. Third, actual caloric intake is compared with minimum required caloric intake based on international nutritional norms for different population groups.

4. Fourth, the food actually consumed by reference group is 'scaled up or down' until it reaches the minimum required level of caloric intake.

5. Finally, the cost of this new scaled food basket is calculated, and represents the food poverty line.

To calculate the overall poverty line an allowance is added for non-food expenditure, based on its share of total expenditure in the reference group. Calculated in this way, the food poverty line represents a minimum level of food expenditure, whereas the total poverty line represents minimal food and non-food expenditure, based on the consumption patterns of a reference group. The approach reflects the Empiricist commitment to brute data and intersubjective observability discussed in Chapter 2.

The final stage in the analysis is the aggregation of those who fall below the poverty line. Most of the empirical studies presented throughout this book rely simply on the poverty headcount, or the percentage of the poor in the total population. There are other poverty indices, such as the industry standard Foster–Greer–Thorbecke (FGT) class of poverty measures, which are used to calculate the poverty gap, or average shortfall from the poverty line, and poverty intensity, which provides a measure of inequality among the poor.

To summarize, the consumption approach relies on probabilistic sampling and standard error estimation to make claims about the representativeness, or external validity, of results. It calculates household level consumption

---

[2] The other nutrition-based approach, the food energy method, is conceptually similar though can yield quite different empirical results (Ravallion and Bidani 1994).

aggregates, based on fixed-response household surveys questionnaires, and adjusts them to facilitate interpersonal comparisons. The poverty line is anchored on nutritional or caloric intake and a number of poverty indices exist to add up those below the line, most notably the poverty headcount.

3.1.2 *The Dialogic Approach*[3]

Four main issues in identification stage of poverty analysis serve to illustrate the range of tools and methods used. As with the consumption approach, the first issue involves site selection or sampling, and associated claims about the representativeness of data. A second issue concerns ways of eliciting locally meaningful definitions of poverty. A third issue involves techniques of identifying relevant households or individuals to facilitate the final issue of ranking them in terms of well-being.

Sampling is usually done purposively such that a limited number of sites are selected which are supposed to reflect various dimensions of difference relevant to poverty. Examples include, agro-ecological zones, remoteness, ethnicity, main livelihood activity, and so forth. Claims that data are representative of a broader population, or external validity, are based on the concept of empirical generalization, which requires a judgement about the typicality of results over a broader population (Hammersley 1992). The basis of such judgements is often quite contested and there are no clear cut rules on how to arrive at them.

Eliciting locally meaningful definitions of poverty lies at the heart of the dialogical approach. Typically, such definitions are generated from dialogic processes such as focus group discussions or semi-structured interviews. As discussed in Section 2.6, participatory poverty assessments (PPAs) have increasingly recognized that dialogic processes and outcomes are influenced by power relationships between participants in dialogue, including the influence of the PPA facilitator. This has led to the development of various techniques to facilitate wider participation including better identification procedures of 'invisible' groups, organization of separate and/ or smaller discussion for marginalized groups, organization of role plays where social roles are exchanged in order to subtly broach issues of power, critical probing of dialogical results, in particular those which reinforce the expectations of the facilitator, and so on. Additional techniques to facilitate a better understanding of poverty may include semi-structured interviews and livelihood analysis, for a greater appreciation of the livelihood patterns of designated groups, seasonal diagramming, for an understanding of the

---

[3] See IIED (1992) and Chambers (1995).

seasonal dimensions of poverty, Venn diagramming, to plot out hierarchical interrelationships between individuals, groups and institutions, and so on.

The third step involves identification of individuals and households for subsequent well-being ranking. The main technique is a social map whereby the spatial layout of the community is drawn beginning with key community landmarks. Next, all households and household members are listed, along with important household characteristics, if relevant. Identifiers of such households are recorded on the map and elsewhere, such as on cue-cards, to facilitate subsequent ranking. Cross-checking and probing is essential to ensure the inclusion of all households, in particular those that are socially marginal or excluded.

The final stage involves ranking village households, or individuals, in terms of locally relevant definitions of poverty and well-being. Typically, a small group of three to five persons is selected who are supposed to represent a range of perspectives within the community. At times, ranking exercises are conducted separately by population groups, such as men and women, to ascertain if results differ according to the rankers. Respondents are asked to divide the population into broad ranking categories such as 'worse off, middle, better-off', and to rank all village households or persons within the assigned categories. The actual ranking is often conducted by sorting cue-cards, each of which represents a separate household. Reasons for the subsequent ranking, along with reasons for disagreement among rankers, are recorded along with the ranking results. On the basis of such results, information on community-specific levels of poverty can be estimated.

In summary, the dialogical approach relies on purposive sampling and empirical generalization to make claims about external validity. It uses dialogical techniques to better understand local definitions of poverty, social maps to identify households or individuals, and well-being ranking techniques to rank them according to their poverty status.

3.2 Do Definitions Matter? Empirical Results

The 'first generation' of Q² analyses examined the empirical relationship between results from dialogic and consumption or income approaches to poverty. Such studies were often inspired by earlier research which brought attention to the wide range of local meanings associated with the term poverty. On the basis of such findings, Robert Chambers, for example, proposed a threefold categorization of deprivation based on consumption for survival, assets for security, and independence for self-respect (Chambers 1988). He later extended this schema, drawing on further PPA results, to include eight main categories: (i) poverty as lack of physical necessities, assets, and income; (ii) social inferiority; (iii) isolation; (iv) physical weakness; (v) vulnerability; (vi) seasonality; (vii) powerlessness; and (viii) humiliation or lack of self-respect (Chambers 1995).

Many of the initial Q^2 studies examined if local conceptions and income/consumption poverty identified the same individuals/households, or characteristics of individuals/households, as poor, and/or if they were generating similar findings with respect to poverty levels and trends. The core conclusion of this body of literature was that systematic differences did in fact exist on all counts. The overlap between populations identified as 'poor' according to different definitions has tended to be quite modest, and there were differences in the characteristics of persons identified as poor. Further, large discrepancies were found with respect to poverty levels and trends. A few examples from this earlier literature illustrate the point.

An oft-cited early study was conducted by N. S. Jodha on a panel of ninety-five households in rural Rajastan, India over the periods 1963–66, 1977–78 and 1982–84 (Jodha 1988). Discussions with villagers led to the development of a number of indicators of socio-economic status which were included in household surveys administered over these time periods. Five categories of indicators were generated, based on (i) reduced reliance on traditional patrons, landlords, and powerful people; (ii) reduced dependence on low pay-off jobs; (iii) improved mobility and availability of cash; (iv) consumption of better quality food; (v) acquisition of consumer durables. Stark differences emerged when comparing farmers' perceptions of change, as evidenced by changes in the value of indicators of these variables, with changes in per capita income. For example, between 1963–66 and 1982–84, households where per capita income had fallen by at least 5% showed very significant improvements in indicators of reduced reliance on a patron, including households with members working as attached labour (37% vs. 7%); households residing on a patron's land (31% vs. 0%); households borrowing off-season foodgrain from patrons (77% vs. 26%), and so on. On the basis of this evidence, Jodha argued that such communities perceived themselves as better off despite falls in income. He further maintained that standard '[standard] concepts and categories used to identify and classify rural realities are too restrictive' and affirmed the 'need for a fresh look at the conceptualizations underlying the measurement of the level and change in rural poverty' (Jodha 1988: 2421, 2427).

In a somewhat similar vein, Ian Scoones (1995) compared the results of household survey data and wealth rankings conducted with seventy-one villagers in rural Zimbabwe in 1986–87. Local criteria of wealth included productive assets, output, and income, consumption, social status as determined by political importance, age and respect, prestige and esteem. Subsequent analysis found importance differences between the wealth ranking and various socio-economic indicators in the survey. For example, correlation coefficients between income and the wealth rankings were statistically significantly but quite modest. In some cases, income levels were actually lower among better off well-being ranking categories. Likewise, there were important differences between groupings of households according to their wealth ranking results and according to cluster analysis which grouped households on the basis of conventional indicators of assets, crop yields, income, and household characteristics. Only twenty-nine of sixty-four households were grouped in the same of four well-being ranks and clusters. Scoones (1995: 85) offered the following explanations for such differences: 'prestige, respect, esteem, conduct, behaviour and local political influence may be significant in ranking a particular household and act to trade-off against potentially lower asset or income levels'.

Bevan and Joireman (1997) compared the results of four approaches to identifying the poor applied to the same population in three sites in rural Ethiopia. The four approaches were based on consumption expenditure, community wealth-rankings, self-reported well-being status from a household survey and cluster analysis drawing on household variables collected in the household survey. In terms of population overlap, the percentage of total households incorrectly ranked by at least one of the four approaches was between 59% and 71% in the three sites. In terms of the comparison between the consumption and wealth-ranking approaches, Spearman rank correlation coefficients were quite low, ranging from 0.18 to 0.26 whereas the percentage of total households incorrectly ranked as poor in the two approaches was between 39% and 62%. In terms of poverty incidence, the respective rates for the consumption and wealth-ranking approaches in the three communities were 12% and 53%, 15% and 77%, and 61% and 76%, respectively. The differences in research results generated by the four approaches led the authors to conclude that 'people can be poor in different ways and for different reasons, and that these need exploring further before they can be meaningfully aggregated using one measure' (Bevan and Joireman 1997: 332).

Shaffer's (1998) study in the Republic of Guinea came to similar findings, drawing on results of a nationally representative household survey and a PPA conducted in one village in the region of Upper Guinea. Data from the former suggested that women were not more likely than men to be consumption poor or to suffer greater consumption poverty. The incidence, intensity, and severity of poverty were higher in male-headed than female-headed households, and females were underrepresented in poor households. In addition, almost all indicators of intrahousehold distribution of food or health care, such as various nutritional outcome and mortality indicators, did not show female disadvantage. Results from dialogical inquiry in the PPA suggested, however, that consumption poverty missed two important aspects of female poverty, namely excessive work load and restricted decision-making authority. In group discussions, a substantial majority of men and women maintained that women were 'worse off' than men, and a larger majority held that in a second life they would prefer to be born male than female. In subsequent well-being ranking exercises, groups of both men and women separately ranked *all but two* married village women below *all but two* male household heads. The group of men explained this ranking primarily in terms of decision-making authority whereas the women used the Malinké phrase *moso ye dyön né di*, which characterizes married women as 'slaves'. The PPA evidence suggests that in Kamatiguia, women are worse off than men when deprivation extends beyond consumption poverty to include a range of items which are 'discursively' explored.

A number of more recent studies have come to broadly similar conclusions as these earlier ones. Wodon (2007), for example, reviewed results of household survey data from West Africa which included standard consumption modules along with 'subjective' questions on perceived changes in poverty in their countries or communities. While the subjective question is dialogic only in the broadest sense of the term, results are nevertheless revealing. As shown in Table 3.1, in all four countries poverty incidence fell between 25% and 11%, yet a substantial majority of respondents felt that poverty had increased or remained constant.

In another example, Levine and Roberts (2008) compared data on levels and trends of poverty using data from national income/expenditure surveys and PPAs in Namibia over the period 2003–4. A number of stark difference emerged between these two sources of data. The former found that overall poverty incidence, defined in terms of a 60% food-share poverty line, fell from around 38% to 28% between 1993/4 and 2003/4. Further, total expenditure and food expenditure increased for all expenditure deciles at the nation level, and in three regions covered by the PPA. By contrast, PPA results suggested much higher levels of poverty in all three communities, between 78%

Table 3.1 Poverty trends in West Africa

	Cameroun	Guinea	Mauritania	Senegal	
	1996–2001	1994–2002	1990–2000	1994–2001	2001–2006
Poverty reduction (%)	25	22	18	16	11
Perceptions of poverty					
Worsening	54	23	31	64	44
No change	17	50	41	13	22
Improvement	17	25	28	19	31

Source: Wodon (2007, Table 1).

and 85%, and decided negative trends in two of three. In such communities, villages made reference to worsening food security due to drought, declining soil quality, overpopulation, and overexploitation of natural resources along with retrenchment of farm workers and food price inflation. Levine and Roberts (2008) explained the findings in terms of three factors which do not necessarily map onto income or consumption poverty, namely a deterioration in asset holdings, reduced access to and quality of basic services, and increasing vulnerability related to food insecurity and AIDS.

Similar results are presented in Lu's (2010, 2011) work from Yunnan Province, China, where four approaches to poverty, the official identification method (based on low-income households identified by village officials), PPA, consumption poverty, and a multidimensional poverty index (MDI),[4] were applied to the same population. Only four of 473 households, or less than 1%, were identified as 'poor' by all approaches. In terms of the comparison between consumption poverty and the PPA, differences emerged with respect to poverty incidence, at 18% and 34% respectively,[5] and concerning certain characteristics of poverty, such as the number of sick household members, where the sign on correlation coefficients differed (Lu 2011: 185, 187). In terms of population overlap, around 52% of consumption poor households were also 'PPA poor', while only 29% of 'PPA poor' households were consumption poor (Lu 2011: 245).

Two further studies affirm this modest overlap of households defined as poor by dialogical and consumption approaches to poverty. Saith's 2000–1 study of around 300 rural and urban households in Uttar Pradesh, India, combined data from a household survey and a PPA administered to the same population (Saith 2007). Interestingly, both approaches identified around one-third of households as poor. In terms of overlap of households, just over half of consumption-poor households were also 'PPA poor' and vice versa. Franco's (2007) study applied a similar methodology in rural and urban settings on the outskirts of Lima, Peru. Focus group discussions pointed to a wide range of locally meaningful aspects of poverty including precarious livelihoods, physical insecurity, social divisions, powerlessness, and so forth. The overlap between households identified as poor was somewhat higher than in the other studies. Around 70% of consumption-poor households were also 'PPA poor' and around 55% of 'PPA-poor' households were also consumption poor.

Three other relevant findings in the empirical literature are worth mentioning because they concern related questions. Certain of these findings, which

---

[4] The MDI included indicators of demographic composition, education, employment, assets, and expenditure.
[5] These figures rely on the national poverty line adjusted to reflect local prices.

show agreement between household survey and wealth-ranking results, do not contradict the previously reported findings because they address different issues. Other findings are broadly supportive of the core conclusion that different approaches to poverty generate different results.

A first strand in the literature compares the findings of household survey and wealth ranking with respect to household asset holdings or characteristics. This type of analysis is not assessing the relationship between different definitions of poverty, but the validity of different methods at estimating household assets and characteristics. Empirical results have been mixed. One study in north-eastern Peru found that both wealth-ranking and household surveys identified the same level of productive capital, shop and household assets in around 80% of cases though this accuracy rate dropped to around 60% for consumer durables (Takasaki *et al.* 2000: 1968–69). A similar type of analysis conducted in Northern Mali found that the two approaches generated significant differences in the average number of carts, ploughs, cattle, sheep, and goats per household but not draft animals (Christiaensen *et al.* 2001: 13–15).

A second type of analysis attempts to assess the validity of PPA wealth-ranking results by analysing whether characteristics of households differ significantly by wealth rank, using household survey data administered to the same population. The core conclusion of this literature is that there are indeed statistically significant differences. One such study in rural Bangladesh, found such differences for all seventeen health, demographic and socioeconomic variables in the household survey when comparing across three wealth-ranking categories. In addition, most of the pairwise comparisons between ranking categories also revealed statistically significant differences (Adams *et al.* 1997: 1169). Another similar study in Tanzania found significant differences across well-being ranks for many, but not all, welfare-relevant variables including number of adult males and agricultural workers, acreage in crops, livestock ownership, and so on (Temu and Due 2000). Such results bolster claims about the validity of wealth ranking techniques in identifying distinct socio-economic groups but do not address the question of whether different approaches identify different population groups as poor.

A final stand in the literature examines the correspondence between different dimensions of poverty drawing exclusively on household survey data. Accordingly, such dimensions of poverty are not dialogically generated but certain of them, such as health, nutrition, and so forth, are often mentioned in dialogical studies. The general conclusion of this literature is that there are wide differences in terms of population overlap, levels, and trends. According to a comprehensive review of this literature (Stewart *et al.* 2007: 236–7):

> Conceptualisation, definition and measurement have important implications for targeting and policy. The considerable lack of overlap empirically between the

different approaches to poverty means that targeting according to one type of poverty will involve serious targeting errors...Definitions do matter.

The overall conclusion, then, of the empirical literature is that definitions do matter. When comparing consumption poverty with locally relevant definitions of poverty known through dialogic processes, differences emerge with respect to poverty levels, trends, and to population characteristics and overlap. The following section further explores potential reasons for this so-called 'micro-macro' paradox.

3.3 Explaining The 'Micro–Macro' Paradox

Why do the results of consumption and dialogical approaches to poverty differ? We have already suggested that a major part of the explanation has to do with the different dimensions of poverty highlighted by the two poverty approaches. There are other potential reasons as well, relating to perverse consumption, population coverage, intrahousehold issues, visibility bias, recall, and nostalgia bias, which will be discussed in turn.

3.3.1 *Different Dimensions of Poverty*

A number of issues fall under this first category of explanation. The most obvious in the literature is simply the fact that consumption poverty does not comprise everything deemed to be of value by local populations. There is no disagreement on this issue. Such omissions include the 'social wage', or the stream of benefits derived from public provisioning of health, education, and so forth (Moore *et al.* 1998; Kanbur 2001). Other dimensions of poverty influencing well-being ranking results include independence and self-respect (Jodha 1988), esteem and political influence (Scoones 1995), fatigue and social standing (Shaffer 1998), vulnerability and insecurity (Chambers 1995), and so forth. The different underlying conceptions of poverty in the two approaches, which stem in part from their different philosophical foundations discussed in Chapter 2, are a primary reason for the discrepant results.

3.3.2 *Perverse Consumption*

A related issue concerns 'welfare-reducing' consumption expenditure items which serve to inflate consumption expenditure. Some of these so-called 'consumption bads' include expenditure on medical expenses, alcohol, and other social vices (McGee 2004). While it has been recommended that such items be removed from the consumption aggregate (Deaton and Zaidi 2002), it is not always standard practice to do so. For example, such 'bads' were not omitted from the consumption estimates in Lu's above-mentioned study, which is one likely reason that the number of sick household members increases with consumption expenditure.

3.3.3 *Population Coverage*

Another potential explanation for discrepant results is simply that the population differs in time or space (Devereux and Sharp 2006). Some of the empirical studies compared results of nationally representative household surveys with studies which were not designed to be statistically representative and which comprised a much smaller number of observations (for example, Shaffer 1998). This same point applies if the reference period for the comparison of well-being trends differs as appears to be in the case in some of Wodon's West African studies discussed above and the comparison of PPA and household survey results in Uganda (McGee 2004).

3.3.4 *Intrahousehold Issues*

Consumption expenditure is collected at the level of the household and adjusted by the number of household members or adult equivalents. As such it can mask inequality in the intrahousehold distribution of consumption, in particular along gender lines. While there are techniques to test for gender discrimination in household consumption (Deaton 1997), these are at multiple removes from the simple poverty comparisons presented above. Accordingly, a worsening of intrahousehold distribution could explain perceptions of worsening conditions, especially for female respondents (McGee 2004).

3.3.5 *Sampling and Price Adjustments*

Household surveys data may be overstating improvements in consumption expenditure, and consequent declines in poverty, in certain cases. Two examples illustrate the point. First, if the sampling frame is not capturing recent rural to urban migrants, and poverty incidence among these households is higher than prior to migration, reductions in poverty will be overstated. There is some evidence of this in Vietnam (Pincus and Sender 2008). Second, it is often the case that price adjustments over time and space do not distinguish between the consumption basket of the poor and others. If the price of the former is rising faster than the latter, consumption increases among the poor will be inflated, and reductions in poverty overstated.

3.3.6 Visibility Bias

In studies where people are asked about their perceptions of overall trends in poverty, and not changes in their own circumstances, an upward bias in poverty trends may be introduced if poverty has become more visible to onlookers. Such enhanced visibility may occur for a number of reasons. First, in the context of positive rates of population growth, poverty incidence may indeed fall, yet the absolute number of poor persons increase (Kanbur 2001). The reason is simply because the overall number of persons has increased, not because poverty incidence is rising. Second, poverty may be more readily observable in urban settings due to the closer physical proximity of urban dwellers and the greater visibility of certain characteristics of urban poverty such as begging or street children (Wodon 2007). In such situations, perceptions of increasing poverty incidence may simply be due to its increasing visibility.

3.3.7 Recall and Nostalgia Bias

Recall is used in fixed response household surveys, focus groups, semi-structured interviews, and so on to collect specific information on consumption expenditure for example, or more general information on changes in overall living conditions. There is a large literature on the potential biases which may arise when using recall, along with the cognitive psychological processes generating them.[6] One form of bias, nostalgia for the past (Morewedge 2012), is a potential explanation for the perception that poverty has increased, and living conditions have worsened, found is certain studies. Evidence consistent with this interpretation is provided by Dercon and Shapiro (2007: 108) drawing on self-reports of well-being status in the 1994 and 2004 rounds of a panel survey in Ethiopia. When asked in 2004 to recall their self-reported well-being status a decade earlier, 29% of households stated that they had been rich or very rich in 1994. In fact, only 7% of respondents categorized themselves as such in 1994, according to the 1994 survey data.

There are very few studies which have attempted to ascertain the relative importance of factors such as these in explaining discrepant results. One recent exception is Davis and Baulch's (2011) study of poverty dynamics in rural Bangladesh. They attempted to explain why findings about expenditure and life-history based poverty transitions differ. The life-histories, which drew on a subsample of households from the household survey, found many fewer escapes from poverty than the expenditure-based approach.

---

[6] Surveys of this literature are found in Sudman *et al.* (1996) and Tourangeau *et al.* (2000).

In reviewing these contrasting findings on a case-by-case basis, the authors concluded that the vast majority of the discrepancies could be attributed to the following four factors: (i) cases where expenditure is a poor proxy of household economic wealth (tested by substituting landholdings for expenditure); (ii) cases where expenditure were very close to the poverty line, and accordingly, poverty transitions reflected very small changes in expenditure which could likely be attributed to measurement error; (iii) cases where other aspects of well-being (including violence, disability, illness or vulnerability) were not captured in the expenditure aggregates; and (iv) cases where a change in household size affected per capita expenditure with little effect on perceptions of well-being (due to the effects of household economies of scale in consumption). According to the authors, the percentage of discrepant cases explained by these four factors was 43%, 30%, 15%, and 11%, respectively. In summary, reliance on different dimensions of poverty, as represented by the first and third explanations, accounted for over half of the contrasting findings between the two approaches.

3.4 Conclusion

It was argued in Chapter 2 that epistemology matters for the way that poverty is conceived and investigated in the consumption and dialogical approaches to poverty. The objective of Chapter 3 was to determine if it also matters for research outcomes. The core conclusion of the review of first-generation Q^2 work is that definitions do indeed matter for the individual households identified as poor, and for certain of their characteristics. It also matters for estimates of overall poverty levels and trends. There are other potential reasons, however, for divergent results between consumption and dialogical approaches relating to population coverage, intrahousehold issues, visibility bias, recall/nostalgia biases, and so on. The one empirical study which has attempted to ascertain the relative importance of different explanations such as these found that differences in definitions of poverty do account for over half of the contrasting findings.

The first-generation Q^2 analyses served the useful purpose of exploring differences between consumption and dialogical approaches to poverty, affirming that definitions matter and the locally meaningful definitions of poverty should figure somewhere in poverty analysis. First-generation analysis did not, however, devote much attention to uncovering optimal ways of combining different research approaches. Nor did it place emphasis on addressing challenges of making consistent interpersonal comparisons and establishing the external validity of research results. It was the second generation of Q^2 analysis which took up these tasks.

Chapter 4[1]

Second-Generation Q²: Addressing Comparability and Validity

It was argued in Chapter 2 that epistemological differences explain different features of the consumption and dialogical approaches to poverty. Further, it was shown in Chapter 3 that different approaches tend to identify different households, with different characteristics, as 'poor' and come to different conclusions concerning poverty levels and trends. The decided emphasis, to this point, has been on difference.

The next stage in the evolution of Q² poverty analysis has been the emergence of analyses aiming to bridge such differences. This chapter presents a selective review of some of these studies, which are referred to as the second-generation of Q² analysis. The format is as follows. First, an organizing framework for the empirical studies is presented in Section 4.1 based on a number of key challenges in the identification stage of poverty analysis. The following three sections, 4.2–4.4, proceed to review empirical studies which address issues related to the chosen dimensions of poverty, the weighting of such dimensions, and the setting of a poverty threshold, respectively. Section 4.5 concludes.

4.1 Tasks and Challenges Facing Q²

As discussed in section 1.4, the identification stage of poverty analysis addresses two main questions: 'Who are the poor?' and 'What are their characteristics?'. It entails a number of tasks which were outlined in Section 3.1 in the discussion of tools and methods of the consumption and dialogical approaches. Three tasks have proved particularly relevant for second generation Q² analyses: (i) operationalizing dimensions of poverty; (ii) outlining their relative weights, if more than one dimension is selected; and

---

[1] A condensed version of parts of this chapter will appear as Shaffer (forthcoming)

(iii) determining an appropriate poverty threshold. Q^2 has made contributions to all three of these activities by addressing four key challenges in the identification stage of poverty analysis.

The first challenge concerns the imperative of including 'locally meaningful' dimensions of poverty in the analysis. Otherwise stated, conceptions of poverty should correspond to people's understanding of the term. The philosophical justification was presented in the discussion of hermeneutics in Chapter 2. A second, related argument, from social anthropology, is that concepts such as poverty, should bear a close relationship to local categories of social differentiation (Green 2006, 2009). Otherwise, 'we' are imposing analytical categories with little local relevance. A final argument comes, perhaps surprisingly, from neo-classical economics which has championed a 'subjective' conception of value, based on individual preferences, as opposed to its predecessor in economics, the labour theory of value (Dobb 1973). Following this logic, one might expect that a similar 'subjectivity' should apply to the valuation of dimensions of poverty, especially for those whose work falls within the applied tradition of (neo-classical) micro-economics. In light of the above, it would be odd if local conceptions of poverty didn't figure *at all* in poverty analysis.

While there are good reasons to incorporate locally meaningful categories in poverty analysis, immediate problems pose with respect to consistent interpersonal comparisons of well-being which are often required for policy purposes. First, if the dimensions of poverty, the 'basket', differ over the range of the comparison, one is not comparing 'like with like'. Accordingly, results of such comparisons raise significant problems of interpretation, given that different objects of value are being compared. Hereafter, we refer to this challenge as that of 'basket' consistency.

Second, even if the 'basket' is the same, perceived levels of fulfilment, or adequacy, of that 'basket', or its commodity requirements, may systematically differ across population groups. The reason is that the reference level of what constitutes fulfilment or adequacy may systematically differ. One example is that richer households often fare worse than poorer ones in self-reports of morbidity because they apply a lower bar of what constitutes illness (Sen 2002). This example is one instance of the broader phenomenon of adaptive preferences or 'sour grapes', which holds that our preferences are shaped by what is attainable so, drawing on Aesop's fable of the *Fox and the Grapes*, the grapes are deemed 'sour' because unattainable (Elster 1987). 'Levels' consistency will be the term used to refer to this challenge, which also refers to the level at which the poverty threshold is set.

It must be recognized that issues related to 'levels' consistency are quite complex and depend on normative judgements about what types of 'level' differences should be 'allowed for' when making interpersonal comparisons of well-being. Some interpersonal differences related to social circumstances (climate, social relationships) or personal characteristics (pregnancy, disability) imply higher commodity requirements to reach the same levels of achievement. By and large, these types of issues, which Amartya Sen (1983, 1999) has addressed at length over the years, are not addressed in the review of Q² studies.

The fourth challenge involves extrapolating results spatially, or establishing external validity, which, once again, may be required for policy purposes. A preliminary distinction was made in Section 3.1 between statistical inference, based on probabilistic sampling, and empirical generalization of purposively sampled dialogical studies. A core objective of many second-generation Q² analyses has been to integrate aspects of dialogical inquiry with probabilistic sampling.

Table 4.1 combines the three elements and four challenges of the identification stage of poverty analysis along with the main categories of Q² contributions. Empirical examples from within each category are reviewed in turn in the sections which follow.

4.2 Operationalizing Dimensions of Poverty

As discussed, first-generation Q² analyses placed emphasis on bringing locally meaningful definitions into the analysis of poverty. A next step in

Table 4.1 Poverty identification: empirical contributions

	Desirable properties			
	Meaningful	Basket consistency	Levels consistency	External validity
Identification				
Specifying dimensions				
i Including locally meaningful definitions in a survey	x	x		x
ii Poverty correlate/dimension mapping	x	x	x	x
iii Statistical adjustment and vignettes	x		x	x
Weighting dimensions				
i The indirect approach	x	n/a	n/a	x
ii The direct approach	x	n/a	n/a	x
Setting thresholds				
i Data discontinuities	x	x		
ii Conceptual thresholds	x	x		x
iii Consumption adequacy question	x			x

x denotes that these issues have been addressed by at least some of the empirical examples which fall under the headings.

the evolution of Q^2 has been to incorporate locally meaningful definitions in the analysis while addressing consistency requirements of interpersonal comparisons, as well as external validity. Three categories of analysis of this type are reviewed, including locally meaningful definitions in a survey, mapping of poverty correlates or dimensions from small n studies to household surveys and statistical adjustment including the use of vignettes.

4.2.1 *Including Locally Meaningful Definitions in a Survey*

A first approach is to standardize locally meaningful definitions and include them in a survey administered to a probabilistically sampled population. An example is provided by Barahona and Levy's (2007) evaluation of the targeting efficiency of Malawi's Targeted Input Program (TIP), which aimed to distribute small amounts of seed and fertilizer to the poorest rural households. The key research question was to determine the coverage of poor households, and leakage to the non-poor, in the targeted distribution scheme. Prior Participatory Rural Appraisal (PRA) wealth rankings, conducted as part of the TIP evaluation highlighted the centrality of food security as a dimension of poverty in rural areas. Based on the detailed narrative information in the PRA, three categories of food security were distinguished: (i) households that have enough to eat throughout the year (*food secure*); (ii) households that have enough food from harvest to Christmas but not after (*food insecure*); (iii) households that have a longer period of not having enough to eat (*extremely food insecure*). Food security, so defined, was subsequently included in a survey instrument administered to all households in villages and regions sampled probabilistically. While the authors acknowledge that such a poverty definition is 'not perfect' they maintained that it was meaningful to participants, easy for households to self-identify into one of the categories, and capable of distinguishing well-being groups of relevance to the study.

This example is partially successful in meeting 'basket' consistency, in that the definition of one locally relevant dimension of poverty, food insecurity, has been standardized and included in a survey instrument administered to a broader population. There is *conceptual* clarity in the idea of 'having enough to eat', in the sense that it has a relatively unambiguous referent. In terms of 'levels', however, there could be systematic differences in terms of both what is perceived to be 'enough' as well as the associated commodity requirements.[2] The implicit assumption appears to be that, across rural Malawi, the population is similar enough to allow for consistent comparisons. External

---

[2] This point is analogous to Sen's (1983) conceptualization of poverty as absolute in the space of capabilities or functionings, such as being adequately nourished, but relative in the space of the commodities required to achieve these functionings.

validity is achieved through the use of probabilistic sampling which facilitates the calculation of standard errors for the estimates of population percentages presented.

A second example is Sharp and Devereux's 2001–2 study of destitution in the Wollo area of Amhara region, Ethiopia (Devereux and Sharp 2006; Sharp 2007). The study employed a two-stage approach to understanding meanings of, and trends in, destitution. In a first exploratory stage, 'qualitative' and 'quantitative' research teams worked jointly to development and refine questions to pose in the study. A second stage entailed the use of tools of participatory rural appraisal in nine sites, along with the administration of a fixed-response household survey to over 2,000 households sampled probabilistically in Wollo. Of primary concern was the inclusion in the household survey of a definition of destitution which was at once comparable across sites yet reflective of local understandings of the term.

The definition of destitution used in the survey was built upon prior conceptual work, drawing on the livelihoods framework, which identified three core constituents of destitution: (i) inability to meet subsistence needs; (ii) lack of access to productive assets; and (iii) dependence on public or private transfers (Devereux 2003). Discussion in the exploratory phase translated this concept into two operational categories, the vulnerable and destitute, defined, respectively, as 'struggling—managing to meet household needs, but by depleting productive assets and/or sometimes receiving support' and 'unable to meet household needs by own efforts, dependent on support from community or government (could not survive with it)' (Sharp and Devereux 2004: 235). These definitions were included in the household survey and respondents asked to self-identify into one of these categories.[3] According to the authors, cross-checking during the participatory work broadly confirmed the local relevance of this definition, in particular the inclusion of an aspect concerning dependence on others for sustenance, which reflected extreme poverty.

As with the Barahona and Levy's study, the core contribution of this study is to incorporate a locally meaningful definition of poverty, or in this case destitution, in a way which is comparable across households or sites. In terms of 'basket' consistency, much hinges on whether household needs are similar across the domain of the comparison. For 'levels' consistency, the same point applies to perceived adequacy levels of needs and their resource requirements. Probabilistic sampling, within Wollo, allow for claims of external validity to be based on estimates of standard errors.

In both of these cases, locally meaningful dimensions of poverty were identified through dialogical processes and subsequently standardized and

---

[3] Two other categories, 'sustainable' and 'viable', were also included.

included in a household survey administered to a probabilistically sampled population. Such studies succeeded in bolstering claims of external validity but require assumptions of relative population homogeneity to meet requirements of 'basket' and 'levels' consistency.

4.2.2 Poverty Correlate or Dimension Mapping

This category is similar to the preceding one in that locally generated dimensions of poverty are used, rather than poverty rankings *per se*, to identify meaningful dimensions of poverty and to facilitate comparisons of 'like with like' with a view to address 'basket' consistency. The main difference is such dimensions are 'mapped' onto existing household survey data rather than included in a survey.

An example is provided by Howe and McKay's (2007) attempt to identify chronically poor households in Rwanda through combined use of data from a 2001 Participatory Poverty Assessment (PPA) and a 1999–2001 national household survey. The methodology is innovative in its attempt to identify chronic poverty on a national level in the absence of panel data, but drawing on findings from a PPA with national coverage. The PPA exercise was a large-scale undertaking covering all districts in Rwanda's twelve provinces. In the province of Butara, all 679 of the lowest administrative unit, cells, were covered. In the remaining eleven provinces, ninety-six of the second lowest administrative unit, sectors, participated (Republic of Rwanda 2001).

Three steps were involved in the overall study. First, analysis of the narrative information in the PPAs suggested that chronic poverty comprised primarily three categories of poor persons, identified in all twelve provinces: those in abject poverty (*Umutindi nyakujya*) who beg to survive; the very poor (*Umutindi*) who work for others; and the poor (*Umukene*) with small landholdings and no savings. Second, characteristics of these three categories associated with persistent poverty in the narrative information were mapped onto indicators contained in the household survey. Three core indicators of chronic poverty were identified: (i) the household's main activity is own account agriculture or agricultural wage labour; (ii) the household cultivates less than 0.05 ha per adult equivalent; (iii) the household does not own livestock. Third, descriptive statistical analysis from the household survey allowed for an estimate of national incidence of chronic poverty so defined along with the relationship between chronic poverty and other variables included in the survey.

As the authors acknowledge, there are certainly errors of exclusion and inclusion in this approach. Nevertheless, it makes a serious attempt at meeting the aforementioned challenges of the identification stage of poverty analysis. First, it relies on locally meaningful definitions of poverty, and chronic poverty, based on locally generated definitions, aggregated across PPA cites with national coverage. Second, by relying on specific correlates of poverty, it allows for interpersonal comparisons of 'like with like', addressing 'basket' consistency. Third, by choosing intersubjective observable indicators of the chronic poverty correlates, the problem of 'levels' consistency does not apply. Fourth, claims of external validity are based on the twin facts that the PPA had national coverage and the household survey used probabilistic sampling. The main question mark, as the authors acknowledge, is the adequacy of the chosen correlates of chronic poverty drawn loosely from the PPA results. It would have been useful to conduct sensitivity analysis, of the type presented in Chapter 3, to determine how much the selection of particular correlates mattered for estimates of chronic poverty incidence.

A second example involves an innovative methodology used in a participatory wealth ranking exercise in eight rural sites in Limpopo Province, South Africa (Hargreaves *et al.* 2007). The authors used the following five-stage process:[4]

i. In a preliminary focus group discussion, participants were asked to identify the characteristics of households who are 'very poor', 'poor but a bit better off', and 'those that are doing ok' which generated categories of *general statements.*

ii. Next, participants ranked all village households into a number of wealth categories of their own choosing and identified characteristics of these different ranking piles, known as *pile statements.*

iii. All statements were coded into different categories and counted according to the frequency with which they were uttered.

iv. *Pile scores* were then assigned to the pile statements based on the frequency with which they were made with respect to a particular wealth category according to the formula in note 5. The more times a statement was made with respect to higher ranking category, the higher the scores assigned.[5]

v. A household wealth index was calculated based on the mean of the pile statement scores for the wealth category into which the household was ranked.

---

[4] A sixth stage, setting the poverty line, is discussed in Section 4.4.

[5] Piles scores were calculated by first creating category scores according to the formula: $100 \times (N - n)/(N - 1)$, where n is the category number and N the total number of categories ($n = 1$ for the lowest category). So, in the case of five ranking categories ($N = 5$), category scores would be 0, 25, 50, 75, and 100. Next, pile scores were calculated according to the formula $ps = (c_{i...j} \times f)/10$, where c is the category score and f the frequency that the pile statement uttered. For example, in the case of five well-being ranking categories, if a statement was uttered eight times with respect to the lowest ranking category and twice for the second lowest category the pile statement score (ps), would equal 5, and be calculated as follows: $ps = [(0 \times 8) + (25 \times 2)]/10$.

Table 4.2 The Hargreaves *et al.* approach

Pile statement			General statement (frequency)			
Score	No	Statement	Very poor	Poor	OK	Threshold
0	7	Don't have soup	10	0	0	Very poor
0	22	No parents	24	0	0	Very poor
0	39	Beg for food	33	0	0	Very poor
2.8	28	No soap	15	0	0	Very poor
3.2	41	Not got shelter	33	0	0	Very poor
3.7	58	No one is working	34	0	0	Very poor
14.4	76	Shacks	18	15	0	Poor
17.3	31	No shoes/barefoot at school	9	4	0	Poor
22.7	64	Bad/poor housing	19	0	0	poor
24	175	Farm employment	0	80	0	PBBO
28.4	145	Selling fruits and vegetables	0	39	0	PBBO
28.7	99	Domestic work	0	45	0	PBBO
80.4	124	Teacher	0	0	10	OK
84.8	162	University/tertiary	0	0	52	OK
87.9	163	Big house	0	0	96	OK

PBBO, 'poor but a bit better off'.

Source: based on Hargreaves *et al.* (2007: 218–221).

Table 4.2 provides an illustration of the results of this approach, including the types of statements uttered, for different wealth-ranking categories.

The strength of this approach is the attempt to reconcile locally meaningful definitions with 'basket' consistency by relying on poverty correlates which are subsequently transformed numerically. As with other examples, 'levels' consistency obtains only if the commodity or resource requirements of the different poverty correlates are similar across the domain of the comparison. For some correlates such as 'don't have soup', 'no soap', 'has no place to sleep', this assumption seems quite reasonable. In this study, no attempt was made to establish external validity given the limited number of sites examined.

The main contribution of the two studies has been to address 'basket' consistency by basing interpersonal comparisons on correlates of poverty. In the second study, such correlates are transformed numerically to facilitate interpersonal comparisons in a more direct way. They do not directly address 'levels' consistency and therefore rely on assumptions about relative population homogeneity in order to make consistent interpersonal comparisons.

4.2.3 *Statistical Adjustment and Use of Vignettes*

The next example takes a different approach to facilitating interpersonal comparisons. Rather than relying on correlates of poverty, the focus is on poverty rankings adjusted to take into account site-specific differences which could be driving results. As such, the emphasis here is placed on addressing 'levels' consistency. An example is provided in Campenhout's (2006) attempt to enhance the comparability of participatory wealth rankings conducted in four villages in rural Tanzania.

The methodology included the following four steps:

i. First, village-specific well-being rankings were converted into scores, equal to the value of the wealth ranking category, divided by the number of categories. So, if four wealth categories were chosen, the poorest category (assigned a value of 1), would score 0.25.

ii. Next, analysis of variance (ANOVA) was conducted which affirmed statistically significantly mean and variance differences across the villages in question.

iii. Third, scores were adjusted to control for village and sub-village-specific effects which could be influencing well-being ranking results. The underlying assumption, as recognized by the author, is that rankings within villages or sub-villages rankings do lend themselves to comparisons across villages, after controlling for village or sub-village effects. The first adjustment was simply to subtract village and sub-village means from household scores, assuming that the transformed scores allow for interpersonal comparisons.

iv. A second adjustment involved estimating a model of subjective welfare based on the wealth-ranking results, with random intercepts for both village and sub-village scores. The residuals in this model were then used as the well-being measure in subsequent analysis of correlates of wealth ranking results. The logic of this adjustment is similar to the previous one, in that both attempt to control for village and sub-village factors which could bias interpersonal comparisons. In this way, the issue of 'levels' consistency is addressed.

By design, the approach does not address the issue of 'basket' consistency, in that it relies on ranking results presumably based on different dimensions of poverty across sites. Further, there is no attempt to establish external validity. Its core contribution is the attempt to address 'levels' consistency on the basis of well-being ranking results. It does so by controlling for differences between villages and subvillages which could be affecting ranking results. The core limitation of the approach is that the village or sub-village level effects may themselves be subject to a 'levels' bias. For example, average levels in poor and rich villages may be identical yet reflect very different levels of achievement. By conditioning on villages or sub-villages, the analysis is 'holding constant' that which should itself be at the core of the adjustment.

A different way of addressing the 'levels' problem is based on the use of vignettes.[6] Vignettes are a series of hypothetical situations or questions which provide an intersubjective referent used to anchor subjective responses on a range of issues. They were pioneered by staff at the World Health Organization's Global Programme on Evidence for Health Policy and Harvard University, in an attempt to improve the comparability of self-reported health outcomes in multi-country surveys (Salomon *et al.* 2001, King *et al.* 2004). They are designed to address 'levels' biases which may occur if say, poorer subgroups systematically overstate their wellbeing status relative to richer populations because their referents are lower as discussed in Section 4.1. Subsequently, they have been used to enhance comparability of self-reports of clinical competence of medical practitioners (Das and Hammer 2005), job satisfaction (Kristensen and Johansson 2008), and political efficacy (King and Wand 2007).

In a recent World Bank study in Tajikistan, vignettes were applied to address potential 'levels' biases in interpersonal comparisons of well-being (Beegle *et al.* 2009). Respondents in a multipurpose household survey were asked to locate themselves on a six-step ladder, with the poorest and the rich occupying the first and sixth steps, respectively. Respondents were also administered vignettes which entailed situating four hypothetical families on this same scale. The vignette families in question differed in their frequency of meat consumption, ability to heat their home and afford secondary education for their children, quality of clothing and land ownership.

The analysis sought to test for a 'levels', or a 'frame-of-reference', bias (FORB), in three ways. First, using an ordered probit model, the authors examined if vignette responses were correlated with household characteristics, which would be expected if FORB existed (as noted earlier, one might expect lower income groups to assign higher ranks to each vignette in the six-point scale). Second, vignette responses were included as dummy variables in subjective welfare regressions to purge the model of the 'levels' bias caused by the use of different scales. Third, responses to the above subjective welfare question were rescaled by taking into account the relationship between one's self-reported score and one's rating of the vignettes. The subjective welfare regressions were then re-run with the rescaled responses as the dependent variable. Interestingly, the authors did not find a significant FORB effect in the earlier analyses.

This type of analysis is one of the few to attempt to systematically address the challenge of 'levels' consistency. The key untested assumption is that vignettes do, in fact, allow for the identification of 'levels' biases by providing

---

[6] Additional information, and sources, on vignettes can be found at the 'anchoring vignette website at: <http://gking.harvard.edu/vign>.

an external referent to calibrate scales used by respondents in self-reports of their subjective welfare. 'Basket' consistency is not addressed in that subjective welfare is based on respondents' differing views of what constitutes poverty. Claims to external validity are based on the probabilistic sampling in the household survey which allows for standard error calculation.

4.3 Weighting Dimensions of Poverty

The second broad issue in the identification stage of poverty analysis concerns weighting dimensions of poverty if more than one is selected. In the broader literature, there are three main ways to do this. First, one can assign weights arbitrarily, or normatively, drawing on the analysts' predilections. One example is United Nations Development Programme's Human Development Index whose main component are weighted equally on grounds, *inter alia*, that all are equally important for human development (Anand and Sen 1997).[7] A second approach is to apply forms of statistical analysis which assign weights based on the correlation structure between the various dimensions of poverty in question. Examples include the use of principal component analysis (PCA) (Filmer and Pritchett 2001) and factor analysis (Sahn and Stifel 2003). The third approach, where Q² analyses have made important contributions, is to use 'locally meaningful' weighting schemes based on people's perceptions of the relative importance of different dimensions of poverty. Such analyses employ either indirect approaches, which attempt to retrieve weights from correlates of poverty, or direct approaches, which simply ask people to supply the weights in question.

4.3.1 *The Indirect Approach*

An example of the indirect approach involves attempts to 'back-out' weights through econometric analysis. One study of thirty-seven villages in rural districts of Kenya, Malawi, Tanzania, and Uganda drew on a dataset which combined wealth-ranking results and household survey data (Kebede 2009). An ordered logit model was estimated with wealth rank (poor, middle, rich) regressed on household characteristics including income, assets, land, number of adults, and housing. The author argues that the resulting coefficients, or elasticities, represent an approximation of the social value accorded to such resources as determinants of wealth-ranking categories, though the value of less visible resources will be biased downwards.

---

[7] Another more recent example is Hayati *et al.*'s (2006) multidimensional poverty index applied to Iran in which all fourteen elements are equally weighted

The approach attempts to integrate statistical analysis of conditional relationships between variables with locally meaningful definitions of poverty as reflected in wealth-ranking results. The main assumption, which would seem to require further support, is that such variables actually entered into the considerations of those engaged in the wealth-ranking exercise. To assess the validity of this assumption, it would have been interesting to compare such results with the reasons given for the categorization of persons into well-being rankings categories. Nevertheless, it represents an innovative attempt to infer locally relevant weights from observable characteristics of well-being ranking groups.

4.3.2 *The Direct Approach*

In the direct approach to eliciting local weights, people are simply asked to rank dimensions of poverty or well-being in terms of their relative importance. The direct approach may involve either sequential or simultaneous ranking. One example of the former involves the construction of a composite poverty index, the 'Human Vulnerability Index (HVI)', for the Maldives drawing on data from Vulnerability and Poverty Assessments (VPAs) carried out in 1997/8 and 2004 (de Kruijk and Rutten 2007). The VPAs were nationally representative surveys which covered all 200 inhabited islands along with the capital city, Male. These surveys asked respondents to rank twelve dimensions of well-being in terms of their perceived priority (with the highest priority assigned the value of 1). These twelve dimensions included indicators of income poverty, electricity, transport, communication, education, health, drinking water, consumer goods, housing, environment, food security, and employment. Rankings were averaged separately for men and women, though gender-disaggregated results ended up being identical, and relative weights calculated for use in the HVI.

A second example of sequential ranking is an approach developed by The *Wellbeing Research in Developing Countries* (WED) project, mentioned in Chapter 1. This project produced the Quality of Life (QoL) questionnaire, which attempted to integrate standardized instruments, such as those in the World Health Organizations' QoL surveys, with open-ended, individualized questionnaires, such as the Global Person Generated Index (Gough and McGregor 2007; Camfield *et al.* 2009). As an example, the development of the WEDQoL questionnaire in Thailand (Woodcock *et al.* 2009) began with a preliminary phase in which respondents from rural and urban communities were asked 'Describe a time when you felt very happy, giving reasons'. The results were codified into fifty-one items in the WEDQoL questionnaire, such as 'having sufficient food every day, water, friends, good relationships, public transport etc.' Respondents then rated these items with respect to their perceived necessity for well-being, on a scale of 0–2, and to their satisfaction with the levels of these items, on a scale of 0–3. The mean or median of such scores provided an indication of the relative importance and attainment of dimensions of poverty/well-being respectively, while disaggregation allowed for sub-population-specific assessment. Additional analysis was performed on the data to assess internal validity.

A drawback of sequential ranking as a means of eliciting weights is that the individual scoring does not necessarily take into account the relative importance of all items jointly considered. Accordingly, individual weights may be biased in any number of ways. One method to address this 'sequential bias' was used in a 2008 study on the relative importance of different literary practices in Mozambique (Esposito *et al.* 2012). Focus group discussions were initially held with a view to elicit a short-list of five literary practices which were most highly valued: (i) signing one's name; (ii) performing simple calculations; (iii) dealing with official documents; (iv) using mobile phones; and (v) helping children with homework. In a subsequent survey, data on household characteristics were first collected. Next, respondents were asked to allocate fifty beans among the five pre-identified literary practices according to their relative importance. Subsequently, statistical analysis was performed to assess the significance of differences among response categories and between populations groups. Further, econometric analysis was performed to examine the conditional relationship between the relative importance of the literary practices and various household-level variables. In terms of the ranking exercise, respondents were forced to simultaneously valuate the importance of all five practices, thus addressing sequential bias. The drawback, as the authors acknowledge, is that the procedure is unable to detect overall differences in valuation levels across persons because each were assigned a fixed number of beans.

All of these examples represent interesting attempts to derived locally meaningful weights for the multiple dimensions of poverty. The issues of levels and basket consistency do not directly apply to the weighting issue.

4.4 Setting Poverty Thresholds

The third broad issue in the identification stage of poverty analysis concerns distinguishing between the poor and non-poor, that is drawing the poverty line. As discussed in Section 3.1, in the consumption approach, the line is typically set at some level of income or consumption expenditure corresponding to a basic amount of caloric intake plus an allowance for non-food consumption (Ravallion 1994). The approach incorporates locally meaningful information in a limited sense, in that the poverty threshold is based on the consumption behaviour of households.[8] Q^2 approaches have attempted to set the poverty line at a point which more fully reflects locally meaningful poverty dimensions and thresholds. At least three broad approaches are found in the literature.

4.4.1 *Data Discontinuities*

The first involves analysis of locally generated data on poverty correlates or characteristics to determine if there are natural breaks which distinguish population groups.[9] The study of Hargreaves *et al.* (2007) mentioned earlier provides an example. As shown in Table 4.2, pile statements scores were listed in ascending order and compared with general statements to determine if particular statements were overwhelmingly made about the poor or very poor. By visual inspection, the authors claim to have identified such breaks in the data which were used to subsequently construct wealth bands (based on pile statement scores) distinguishing the poor from the other groups.[10] While more formalized statistical methods exist to detect structural breaks in the data, or populations with similar characteristics, visual inspection can be informative in cases of stark differences between groups. The approach combines a locally meaningful cut-off with 'basket' consistency, facilitated by the reliance on poverty correlates/characteristics rather than ranking results. It does not explicitly address 'levels' consistency which would result only if the commodity or resource requirements of the different poverty correlates are similar.

4.4.2 *Conceptual Thresholds*

A second approach involves use of locally generated poverty definitions which incorporate a 'built-in' conceptual cut-off. The Barahona and Levy (2007) study, discussed earlier, is an example. The well-being measure used in their survey, derived from PRA studies, was food security, defined as 'not having enough to eat' over a specified period. The cut-off is locally meaningful in that it figured prominently in the narrative information in the PRA

---

[8] Some methods of drawing the poverty line, such as variants of the cost-of-basic needs approach, rely on the analyst's judgement to identity a bundle of basic needs goods and do not rely on actual consumption behaviour of the population in question (Boltvinik 1998).

[9] There are similarities here with other attempts to base the poverty line on outcome thresholds, in terms of nutritional outcomes for example, which forms the basis of Lipton's distinction between the poor and the ultrapoor (Lipton 1988).

[10] As such, there are similarities to Townsend's (1979) work on poverty where he estimates, by visual inspection, a poverty line in the UK at 150% of the Supplementary Benefit. At this point, the slope in the relationship between the log of income and the value of a composite deprivation index changes abruptly.

studies. As discussed, the idea of 'having enough to eat' provides a conceptual foundation for 'basket' consistency though, in terms of levels, the associated commodity or resource requirements may differ across populations. External validity is achieved through the use of probabilistic sampling which allows for the calculation of standard errors.

4.4.3 *The Consumption Adequacy Question*

A third approach by Pradhan and Ravallion (2000) and colleagues at the World Bank (Lokshin *et al.* 2006) involves incorporation of a consumption adequacy question in households surveys, whereby respondents are asked if their level of consumption (food, housing, clothing, etc.) is more than, less than, or just adequate to meet family needs. By regressing responses to the consumption adequacy question (CAQ) on consumption expenditure, along with other variables of interest, subjective poverty lines are calculated which reflect the level of consumption expenditure associated with perceived consumption adequacy. More specifically, an ordered probit model is run which estimates the probability of adequately meeting perceived consumption needs conditional on relevant household characteristics. Versions of the basic approach can be used to estimate food poverty and total poverty lines, though the latter entails inclusion of responses about the adequacy of non-food items, as well as the estimation of other components of non-food expenditure. The approach represents a systematic attempt to provide a locally meaningful threshold for a consumption definition of poverty. By definition, it does not address the 'basket' or 'levels' challenges, though the integrated database allows for an estimate of the magnitude of the latter effect. External validity is met by the probabilistic sampling structure of the household survey.

4.5 Conclusion

The first generation of Q² analysis made a strong case that different approaches to poverty lead to the identification of different households as poor and the estimation of different levels and trends of poverty. The second generation of Q² analysis attempted to bridge such differences by incorporating locally meaningful definitions, weights, and thresholds of poverty into the analysis in ways that addressed concerns of interpersonal comparisons and external validity. As such, it tried for the 'best of both worlds'.

This chapter has presented a selective review of the literature of second-generation Q² empirical studies. A wide range of analytical techniques and methodological approaches have been presented many of which have attempted to address issues of 'basket' and 'levels' consistency for interpersonal comparisons and to use probabilistic sampling as the basis of claims of external validity. All of the approaches presented have limitations but they nevertheless represent advances over first generation Q^2 analysis. Further, and importantly, they add value when compared with any approach conducted in isolation by broadening the field of inquiry and frame of analysis. As such, they have contributed to enriching the understanding of the core questions in the identification stage of poverty analysis, namely 'who are the poor and what are their characteristics'.

Part III

Causal Analysis:
Why are People Poor?

Chapter 5

Foundations: Causation and Causal Inference

Part II of this book addressed issues in the identification stage of poverty analysis which asks 'Who are the poor and what are their characteristics?'. Part III focuses on the causal stage of poverty analysis which asks, 'Why are people poor?' I argue that Q^2 approaches have been instrumental in answering this question by providing a more complete understanding of the underlying causal system which produces poverty. The applied argument is presented in Chapters 6 and 7, which review empirical examples of value-added.

The theoretical argument is presented in this chapter which first argues for causal pluralism and then outlines a number of concepts of causation and models of causal inference with relevance to the empirical chapters.[1] The format is as follows. A case for causal pluralism is presented in Section 5.1, which maintains that there is an inherent complexity to the idea of causation which is not adequately handled by any one approach. Sections 5.2, 5.3, and 5.4 proceed to outline three such approaches, namely conditional association, counterfactual dependence, and mechanism-based approaches, respectively. Section 5.5 concludes.

5.1 Causation: 'One Word, Many Things'

The title of this section is taken from an article written by philosopher of science Nancy Cartwright (2004), reprinted in her book *Hunting Causes and Using Them* (Cartwright 2007). Cartwright has argued persuasively that there is no singular concept of causation, or model of causal inference, that does justice to the wide varieties of causal phenomena in the world. Her core argument is that accounts of causation must be substantively different for

---

[1] Parts of this chapter are based on Shaffer (2011).

different causal systems and accordingly, models of causal inference should be specific to the phenomenon under examination. As she phrases it:

> Causation...is a highly varied thing. What causes should be expected to do and how they do it—really, what causes are—can vary from one kind of system of causal relations to another...Correlatively, so too will the methods for finding them. (Cartwright 2007: 2)

The argument presented in Part III of this book extends Cartwright's reasoning. It maintains that there are different conceptions of causation, and associated models of causal inference, which may fruitfully be applied to facilitate explanation of different dimensions of the same phenomenon, such as poverty. Combining approaches to causal inquiry can serve to illuminate different aspects of the underlying causal structure and relationships and, in principle, enrich causal analysis. Whether or not such causal pluralism succeeds in practice is an empirical question, which is addressed throughout Chapters 6 and 7. The theoretical case for causal pluralism, however, requires examining what it means for something to cause something else.

A first point to note is that there are a vast range of theories of causation which provide different accounts of the meaning of causation. Schaffer (2008) lists the following bases for making causal claims: nomological subsumption, statistical correlation, counterfactual dependence, agential manipulability, contiguous change, energy flow, physical processes, and property transference. Similarly, Cartwright (2007) contrasts at least six empirical models of causal inference, including Bayes-nets accounts and Granger causality, modularity accounts, manipulation accounts, invariance accounts, and causal process theories.[2] A *prima facie* case for causal pluralism is simply the co-existence of this wide variety of approaches to causation, all of which have well known strengths and limitations.

There is a core intuition about the meaning of causation, however, which provides a way of navigating among the wide array of approaches. This intuition distinguishes between two concepts of causation, which may alternatively be phrased as 'difference-making and production' (Godrey-Smith 2011), 'dependence and production' (Hall 2004), or 'probabilities and processes' (Schaffer 2008). According to Schaffer (2008):

> The nomological, statistical, counterfactual and agential accounts [of causation]...understand connection in terms of probability: causing is making more likely. The change, energy, process and transferring accounts [of causation] converge in treating connection in terms of process: causing is physical producing

---

[2] Little (1991) adds to this list in his discussion of strategies of causal inference used in the social sciences.

The meaning of the claim that 'a causes b' can indeed turn on our intuitions about 'difference-making' versus 'production' as a depiction of the causal relationship.

The distinction is quite integral to Q^2 causal analysis, in that it lies at the core of differences between processes and outcomes, and between results and mechanisms, discussed in Chapters 6 and 7, respectively. It is useful to present a number of hypothetical examples which illustrate how these conflicting intuitions about the meaning of causation can lead to very different causal inferences. The examples are drawn from Hall (2004), who has provided the most detailed account of this issue.

The first example is a case of production without difference-making. Difference-making is here understood as counterfactual dependence, which is further discussed in Section 5.3. The core idea is that if 'a causes b' then 'b would not have occurred in the absence of a'. Consider a case of 'overdetermination by pre-emption'. Suzy and Billy are engaged in rock-throwing with the objective of shattering a glass. Both throws are perfect, though Suzy's arrives a split second before Billy's and breaks the glass, thereby 'pre-empting' Billy's glass shattering throw. In terms of difference-making, Suzy's throw makes no difference to the glass-breaking as Billy's throw would have shattered it anyway. In terms of physical production, Suzy's throw does indeed cause the glass to break.[3]

A second example presents the converse situation, difference-making without production. Consider a case of double prevention, whereby a forest fire occurring in June was preceded by April rains, which themselves prevented a forest fire in May. Are the April rains a cause of the forest fire in June? Arguably, they are causally related on a 'difference-making' account, in that the June forest fire would not have occurred in the absence of the April rains. They are not so, however, on a production-based account in that they play no role in producing or generating the forest fires.

Hall has argued that the differences between the two concepts of causation are rooted in different underlying principles which characterize them. Production-based accounts are closely related to the notions of transitivity and locality. The first holds that if 'a' causes 'b', and 'b' causes 'c', then 'a' is a cause of 'c'. The last one maintains that causes and effects are linked by a continuous series of intermediate events linked in time and space. Difference-making approaches, on the other hand, rely on counterfactual dependence, as defined above, and allow for the causal effect of omissions, or the failure of an event to occur.

---

[3] The issue is considerably more complex as there are ways to attempt to salvage a difference-making account of causation in this case. Hall (2004) argues that such attempts are ultimately unsuccessful.

What does this have to do with causal analysis of poverty or causal analysis in impact assessment? Consider the hypothetical of two micro-credit projects, *'a'* and *'b'*, which together supply credit to all members of a population.[4] Access to credit from project *'a'* precludes, that is 'pre-empts,' access to project *'b'* and vice versa. Assume that both projects, and not other factors, succeed in significantly raising income, *'c'*, of project participants in identical fashion. In this example, project *'a'* causes *'c'* in terms of 'production', in that it increased the income of project participants, but not in terms of 'difference-making', in that project *'b'* produced identical results.

These issues are not simply hypothetical but have real-world relevance for causal analysis in impact assessment. They are at the root of debates about substitution bias, as exemplified by the following exchange between Thomas Cook and James Heckman:

> It makes little sense to criticize [random assignment] for substitution bias, asserting that, for instance, individuals in the control group had access to services like those to which the treatment group had access. After all, experiments answer the question of whether a treatment is better than some alternative. In this case, the alternative is whatever other services are available…(Cook 2000: 79)

> …the job training experiment Cook mentioned actually killed the large-scale Job Training and Partnership Act (JTPA) program because of what we call substitution bias. Subjects who were randomized out of the study had excellent substitutes for the program, resulting in a gross underestimation of the program's effectiveness. (Heckman 2000: 83)

While this exchange is phrased in terms of the correct counterfactual to use, it can alternatively be interpreted as a debate as to whether or not the impact of a programme should be assessed in terms of difference-making or in terms of some notion of production.

A second case for causal pluralism, then, rests on different intuitions about the meaning of causation, and attendant difference in models of causal inference. Sections 5.2–5.4 extend this discussion by examining differences between two examples of difference-making, conditional association and counterfactual dependence, and one example of production, mechanism-based approaches. There are three preliminary points to note about this discussion.

First, the three approaches to causation were selected on the basis of their relevance to the Q^2 studies reviewed in Chapters 6 and 7. Further, the treatment of issues within each section is closely related to applied issues which arise in causal analysis of poverty and in impact assessment. Accordingly, the

---

[4] This discussion is based on Shaffer (2011).

discussion is partial and addresses only a subset of issues which fall under the relevant headings.

Second, the three approaches in Sections 5.2–5.4 are presented as exemplars of alternative concepts of causation with a view to highlight differences. It must be recognized, however, that there is hybridity within, and overlap between, approaches. For example, applied instances of counterfactual dependence, such as randomized controlled trials (RCTs), present certain types of information on causal mechanisms, as discussed in Section 5.3. Further, some mechanism-based approaches rely on counterfactual dependence to underpin claims about the effectiveness of mechanisms (Glennan 2011). In addition, counterfactual analysis may appear in conditional association, such as econometric models, by say inclusion of a variable for programme participation. Nevertheless, different forms of causal reasoning do tend to characterize ideal types of each of these approaches, despite this hybridity.

Third, most of the applied examples of Q^2 analyses in Chapters 6 and 7 illustrate how different concepts of causes and models of causal inference can be combined to provide a fuller analysis of causation. Accordingly, they differ from the hypothetical cases presented above which focused on how such different approaches may lead to conflicting assessments about the causal effect of particular variables. Nevertheless, both constitute supporting arguments in favour of causal pluralism, from the perspectives of applied methods and theory.

5.2 Conditional Association

Conditional association is the approach to causation which underpins most causal analysis of poverty in the applied micro-econometric tradition. Econometrics, which is simply multivariate regression analysis, is further discussed in this section. Conditional association is closely related to, but not the same as, probabilistic theories of causation.[5] Nevertheless, such theories provide a good entry point for the discussion in that the logic of conditional causation in the econometric context is very similar to that of probabilistic causation *tout court*. Accordingly, we will begin with a general discussion of probabilistic theories of causation followed by a discussion of conditional association in the applied context of the econometrics of poverty.

---

[5] Probabilistic causation is not the same as conditional association because many other approaches to causation are probabilistic. Further, probabilistic causation was not fully integrated into econometrics until Haavelmo's seminal paper, 'The Probability Approach in Econometrics' in 1944. Early econometricians relied on the conditional character of multivariate regression as the basis of their causal claims, and considered their work, in fact, to approximate controlled experiments (Morgan 1990).

The first comprehensive probabilistic theories of causation were developed independently by Reichenbach (1956) and Suppes (1970).[6] The core intuition of these theories is that causes raise the probability of their effects. The relationship may be represented in formal notation as:

$$P(b \mid a) > P(b \mid \sim a),$$

which states that the conditional probability of b given a, is higher that the unconditional probability that b occurs.

Of the many challenges which arise for probabilistic accounts of causation, three are particularly relevant. The first concerns spurious correlations due to common causes. For example, the correlation between falling barometric readings and the occurrence of a storm is spurious in that both are due to a prior fall in atmospheric pressure. To deal with the problem of common causes, a 'no screening off' proviso is added to the core definition. In terms of the above example, atmospheric pressure will 'screen off', or render insignificant, the effect of falling barometric pressure on the probability of a storm. Probabilistic causation then becomes:

i. $P(b \mid a) > P(b \mid \sim a)$.
ii. There is no further event or variable, c, that screens b off from a.

The issue of common causes leads to the second more general challenge facing probabilistic causation: how to determine the events or variables to include in the set of factors which should be 'conditioned upon', or held 'fixed'. At least two specific problems pose. First, conditioning on certain types of variables, causal intermediaries, will illegitimately 'screen off' the effect of underlying or distal causes. Assume, for example, that the causal relationship between smoking and cancer is transmitted solely through the casual intermediary of tar in the lungs. When controlling for tar in the lungs, the effect of smoking becomes insignificant in that the probability of lung cancer is not affected by the source of tar in the lungs. To avoid this problem the set of conditioning variables must be restricted to independent or exogenous variables.

Second, the failure to condition on relevant events or variables can give rise to the so-called 'Simpson's Paradox', whereby a cause does not raise the probability of its effects. Consider, for example, the relationship between smoking (a), heart disease (b), and exercise (c), in situations where smokers are more inclined to exercise, and the effect of exercise on heart disease outweighs that of smoking. In this case, smoking reduces the probability of

---

[6] This discussion is based on Hitchcock (2002 and 2010).

heart disease $P(b\,|\,a)<P(b\,|\,\sim a)$ until one conditions upon exercise, in which case the probabilistic result reverses, such that $P(b\,|\,a\&c)>P(b\,|\,\sim a\&c)$ and $P(b\,|\,a\&\sim c)>P(b\,|\,\sim a\&\sim c)$.

A third broad challenge facing probabilistic causation concerns the direction of causality (Hoover 2008). Even if the complete universe of control variables has been selected, the conditional correlation of a and b does not indicate the direction of causality, nor rule out the possibility of simultaneous or bi-directional causation. The problem is one of observational equivalence, in that the observed correlations are consistent with differing accounts of causal direction. In some cases, the temporal order of events may be used to guide inferences about causal direction, though in practice causal variables may not be temporally ordered and/or effects may be simultaneously determined.

What does this have to do with applied econometric analysis of poverty? The types of problems facing probabilistic causation pose equally for econometric analysis. In econometrics, the causal effect of a variable is estimated after conditioning on, or controlling for, all other independent, exogenous variables in the model. In the context of applied econometrics, if a variable is found to be statistically significant in such modelling, it is often given a causal interpretation as a 'determinant' of the dependent variable. This is certainly the case for econometric modelling of poverty status or dynamics, as reviewed in Chapter 6.

The underlying problem, for all of these three challenges to probabilistic causation, is inferring causation from conditional associations. Hoover (2008) has identified four major ways to address this problem in econometrics. He proposes a 2×2 matrix which distinguishes between approaches that rely on information about the underlying causal system or temporal ordering, on the one hand, and those that include *a priori* or empirical information, on the other. In the quadrant representing temporal ordering and empirical information, one finds 'Granger-causality', whereby the lagged values of regressors are included in the model and interpreted causally, or 'Granger-causally', if found to be statistically significant. Our focus is on those approaches which rely on information about the underlying causal system in question drawing on either *a priori* or empirical knowledge.

The '*a priori*-causal system' tradition, associated with work of the Cowles Commission in the 1940s and 1950s, argued that information on the causal system originates primarily from economic theory. The purpose of econometric analysis is to estimate parameter values for the theoretically derived variables and conduct empirical tests of theoretically derived hypotheses. This position was famously articulated in Koopmans' 1947 paper, entitled

'Measurement without Theory', which critically assessed the methodological basis of the business cycle analyses of Burns and Mitchell (1946). According to Koopmans (1947), such analyses consisted of simple empirical descriptions of the nature of business cycles uniformed by prior economic theorizing about how business cycles work (Morgan 1990).

The 'empirical-causal system' tradition, on the other hand, relies on empirical information to identify the underlying system of causal relationships. A classic statement is Simon's (1953) argument for the use of information from natural or controlled experiments to make inferences about the direction of causality, an approach which has been generalized by Hoover (1990).[7] A more recent trend within this tradition involves the use of instrumental variables to make inferences about the underlying causal relationships (Angrist *et al.* 1996). As further discussed in Section 6.5.1, instrumental variable techniques address problems of reverse causation which may bias econometric results and potentially overturn purported causal effects.

There are two central points of relevance for the discussion of Q^2 approaches to causal analysis in Chapters 6 and 7. First, conditional association within an econometric framework is an approach to causation whose results may be combined with those of other approaches to causation. Examples are presented in Section 6.3.1 on combining outcomes and processes in causal analysis of poverty status. Second, one of the important contributions of Q^2 analyses has been to provide information on the underlying causal system to help infer causes from conditional associations. Selection of exogenous variables, specification of their interrelationships and uncovering instrumental variables are all examples discussed in Section 6.5 of the following chapter.

5.3 Counterfactual Dependence

Counterfactual dependence is an approach to causation which underpins experimental and quasi-experimental approaches to impact assessment.[8] The main difference between the two, as discussed in this section, is that in experimental approaches, such as RCTs, assignment to project and control groups is random, while in quasi-experiments comparisons groups are constructed statistically. The core intuition of counterfactual dependence is that for a to cause b, b would not have occurred in the absence of a (Menzies 2008). In the language of impact assessment, the causal claim that project a

---

[7] The test involves uncovering an event which affects the conditional distribution of some variable, a, without affecting the marginal distribution of another variable, b, in which case it can be inferred that causation does not run from a to b (Hoover 2008).

[8] The discussion in this section is based on Shaffer (2011).

causes outcome *b*, depends on the counterfactual claim about what would have happened to *b* in the absence of *a*.

Proponents of RCTs and quasi-experiments expressly invoke counterfactual dependence in their framing of the core causal question. With respect to RCTs, Duflo *et al.* (2008: 3899) write: 'Any attempt at drawing a causal inference…requires answering essentially counterfactual questions: How would individuals who participated in a program have fared in the absence of the program?' Likewise, the 'archetypal evaluation problem' in the context of quasi-experiments has been phrased as follows: 'an "impact evaluation" assesses a program's performance in attaining well-defined objectives against an explicit counterfactual, such as the absence of the program' (Ravallion 2008: 3789).

The specific causal model underlying experimental and quasi-experimental approaches to impact assessment is known as the Holland–Rubin framework in reference to seminal papers by its authors (Rubin 1974; Holland 1986).[9] The intellectual debt to this framework is explicitly acknowledged by proponents of experiments (Duflo *et al.* 2008) and quasi-experiments (Ravallion 2008). There are three features of the Holland–Rubin model which are particularly germane for the discussion of Q^2 approaches to impact assessment.

First, the analytic focus is on causal effects, not on causal mechanisms. Establishing causal claims, or showing programme impact, rests on differences in the value of outcome/impact indicators between treatment and control/comparison groups. Holland (1986: 945) is very explicit about this emphasis and provides a rationale:

> Others are interested in understanding the details of causal mechanisms. The emphasis here will be on *measuring the effects of causes* because this seems to be a place where statistics, which is concerned with measurement, has contributions to make.

It should be recognized that there is a sense in which applied counterfactual approaches in impact assessment, such as RCTs, provide an account of causal mechanisms. By randomizing assignment to different components of a project, it is possible to infer which sub-components, or causal intermediaries, are and are not effective in producing results. For example, in a micro-credit project, random assignment could occur at the level of initial receipt of funds or at subsequent states in project implementation such as provision of support services. Such causal intermediaries provide a limited account of mechanisms, however, and contrasts sharply with 'thicker' accounts found in the broader literature, as discussed in Section 5.4.

Second, causal effects must be intersubjectively observable. The fundamental problem of causal inference is defined as a problem of observation.

---

[9] Rubin and Holland formalized and popularized the model, which has earlier origins.

Specifically, the same person, household, village, etc., cannot partake in both treatment and control groups simultaneously and, as such, differences in outcomes between treatment and controls cannot be observed. According to Holland (1986: 947): 'It is impossible to *observe* the value of Yt (u) and Yc (u) on the same unit, therefore, it is impossible to observe the effect of t on u. The emphasis is on the word *observe* [original emphasis].' As discussed in Section 2.3, this commitment to intersubjective observability is quite integral to the epistemological tradition of Empiricism.

Third, the key objective of the approach is to provide an estimate of the relative magnitude of causal effect. In the Holland–Rubin framework, causal effect is relative by definition. This is because a causal claim requires a comparison of outcomes between treatment and control or comparison groups. According to Holland (1986: 946): 'The effect of a cause is *always* relative to another cause. For example, the phrase "A causes B" almost always means that A causes B relative to some other cause that includes the condition "Not A"'.

What is the relationship between the Holland–Rubin Framework on the one hand, and experimental and quasi-experimental approaches to impact assessment on the other? Both represent applied attempts to operationalize the concept of counterfactual dependence with a counterfactual model of causal inference (Scriven 2008: 15). As such, they provide a solution to the core challenge facing counterfactual accounts of causation, that, *counterfactuals* are 'possible worlds' or 'unactualized possibilities' which, by definition, do not occur.[10] 'Possible' worlds are rendered 'real' through the use of control or comparison groups and causal claims are based on the logic of the Holland–Rubin framework. As Glymour (1986: 965) phrases it, in reference to the Holland–Rubin model:

> Counterfactual accounts of causality have the disadvantage that they appeal to...possible worlds we will never see...The mystery surely has a solution...we are able to infer counterfactual truths because we make assumptions that we test against one another in rather indirect ways.

There are three central points of relevance for the discussion of Q^2 approaches to impact assessment. First, as discussed in Section 5.1 above, estimates of the magnitude of impact in the Holland–Rubin framework may differ systematically from those in production-based approaches to causation because the former are relative to any number of counterfactual scenarios while the latter are based on what happened over time due to the project. Second, counterfactual dependence is a concept of causation, and model of causal inference, whose results may be combined with those of

---

[10] A large part of the philosophical literature on counterfactual dependence, in particular the work of David Lewis (1973), focused on making sense of this notion of 'possible worlds' and spelling out the associated truth conditions.

other approaches to causation, such as mechanism-based approaches, as illustrated in Section 7.2. Third, Q² approaches have added value by retaining the logic of counterfactual dependence, but dropping the requirement of intersubjective observability, through the use of thought experiments as described in Section 7.4.

5.4 Mechanism-based Approaches

Conditional association and counterfactual dependences are 'difference-makers', to use the terminology of Section 5.1. Causal effect is attributed if associations are uncovered between dependent and independent variables after controlling for all other causal factors determining outcomes or project participation. Mechanism-based approaches, on the other hand, are based on production. Causal inference depends upon identifying the causal mechanisms generating causal effects. According to Little (1998: 202): 'To assert that A's are causes of B's is to assert that there is a typical causal mechanism through which events of type A lead to events of type B.' Mechanism-based approaches figure prominently in those approaches to causation which rely on dialogical and mapping techniques, for example, to make causal inferences.

There is no consensus in the literature as to the precise definition of causal mechanism. In the philosophical literature, mechanisms have been defined alternatively as causal entities and their attendant properties, the causal activities undertaken by such entities or causal processes (Machamer *et al.* 2000). A further distinction contrasts singular causal processes involving multiple linkages in a causal chain and mechanical systems which generate stable and regular causal sequences (Glennan 2011).

In the social sciences, causal mechanisms have been defined in an even greater variety of ways (Hedström and Swedberg 1998; Pickel 2004). Mahoney (2001) has identified at least twenty-four definitions of the term, which he classifies into three broad categories, namely sets of intervening variables linking causes and effects,[11] mid-level theories which provide information about particular elements of higher-level theories, and unobserved entities which have causal effects. More specifically, mechanisms have been defined to include rational choice theories, cognitive processes such as self-fulfilling prophesies, wishful thinking, adaptive preferences, and so on (Elster 1998), functionalist analyses at the level of individuals (Steel 2011) or societies (Cohen 1978), game theory, and so forth (Hedström and Swedberg 1998).

---

[11] Further to the discussion in Section 5.3, RCTs primarily provide information on mechanisms in this first sense of the term.

In the context of applied poverty analysis and impact assessment, mechanisms typically refer to the causal processes generating observed outcomes. Processes comprise the causal variables, the links or pathways between them, that is the causal 'tree', as well as an explanation of why they are linked. Mechanisms, in this sense, focus on the reasons for observed outcomes. Their primary contribution is to shed light on the 'how' and 'why' questions surrounding causal effect.

An example serves to convey the core idea at hand. Sufficient evidence of a causal link between smoking and cancer was provided by the discovery of the mechanisms, or the causal variables and pathways, through which chemicals compounds in tobacco contribute to cancerous cell subdivision and growth. To quote at length from one depiction of these mechanisms (Johnson n.d.):

> Scientists studying a tumor suppressor gene called p53 demonstrated a direct link between cigarettes and lung cancer....When it detects DNA damage, p53 halts cell division and stimulates DNA repair enzymes that fix the trouble. p53 is inactivated in 70% of all lung cancers. A puzzling discovery was that the p53 mutations in cancer cells almost all occur at one of three 'hot spots' within the p53 gene. The key link that explains the 'hot spots' and links lung cancer to cigarettes is a chemical called benzo (a) pyrene (BP), a potent mutagen released into cigarette smoke from tars in the tobacco...[which] binds directly to the tumor suppressor gene p53 and mutates it to an inactive form. The key evidence linking cigarette smoking and cancer, the 'smoking gun,' is that when the mutations of p53 caused by BPDE from cigarettes were examined, they were found to cluster at precisely the same three specific 'hot spots' seen in lung cancers! The conclusion is inescapable: the mutations inducing lung cancer are caused by chemicals in cigarette smoke. Faced with this new incontrovertible evidence, the tobacco companies have abandoned their claim that cigarettes have not been shown to cause cancer.

In the above terminology, the relevant causal variables are the chemicals components in tobacco (BP/BPDE) and the p53 gene, specifically the three 'hot spots on it'. The causal pathway and explanation of linkages includes the (i) release of BP in cigarette smoke; (ii) binding of BP on the three hot spots on the p53 gene; (iii) mutation of the p53 gene rendering it unable to suppress cancerous cell division.

The main point of relevance for the discussion of Q^2 approaches to causal analysis of poverty and to impact assessment is that mechanism-based approaches complement those based on 'difference-making'. The latter have focused on the magnitude of effects, the 'how much' questions, while the former on the underlying reasons, the 'how' and 'why' questions. One of the key contributions of Q^2 has been to combine such approaches to provide a more comprehensive overall account of the causal system in question.

5.5 Conclusion

Causal analysis of poverty addresses the question 'Why are people poor?'. It has been argued that there are a variety of approaches to causation which can contribute to answering this question. More broadly, the chapter presented a theoretical case in support of causal pluralism which is complementary to the empirical case based on the value-added of Q^2 studies reviewed in Chapters 6 and 7.

The theoretical case rests on the inherent complexity of causation, encapsulated in Cartwright's phrase that causation is 'one word, many things'. It further draws on the wide array of conceptions of causation and models of causal inference found in the literature. Among this wide range of approaches, a core distinction is drawn between those which are 'difference-making' and those which are 'producers.' The distinction is important because it corresponds to two core intuitions about the meaning of causation and because it is closely related to differences between approaches found in the empirical Q^2 literature.

Three such approaches to causation were discussed, namely conditional association and counterfactual dependence, which are 'difference-makers', and mechanism-based approaches, which are 'producers'. The first two approaches constitute the foundations of econometric models of poverty and experimental or quasi-experimental approaches to impact assessment, respectively. The latter is the underpinning of those empirical approaches which base causal claims on the mechanisms generating causal effects, relying on relying on theory or people's perceptions.

Understanding causal foundations is important, then, because it explains how we understand, and go about answering, the question 'Why are people poor?'. But how are the different approaches to causation used in practice and what sorts of answers do they provide to this question? Do Q^2 analyses add value in practice and help make an empirical case for causal pluralism? It is to these issues which we turn in Chapter 6.

Chapter 6

Q² Causal Analysis: Exploring the Drivers of Poverty Status and Dynamics[1]

Chapter 5 prepared the groundwork for addressing questions in the causal stage of poverty analysis by reviewing different conceptions of causation and models of causal inference. This chapter examines the empirical application of such conceptions and models with emphasis on 'conditional association' and 'mechanism-based' approaches to causation. Applied examples of counterfactual dependence are discussed in Chapter 7 on impact assessment.

The organizing framework for the presentation of the empirical examples of Q² causal analysis is outlined in Section 6.1 and based on characteristics of the causal framework. Next, the core distinction between poverty status and poverty dynamics is elaborated upon in Section 6.2, along with the related distinctions between stocks and flows of poverty and between chronic and transitory poverty. Section 6.3 proceeds to review empirical examples of the causal analysis of poverty status, specifically those which combine outcomes and processes (Section 6.3.1) along with the rural livelihoods approach (Section 6.3.2). Examples of the causal analysis of poverty dynamics are then presented in Section 6.4 focusing on 'interviewing' the transition matrix (Section 6.4.1) and the 'Stages of Progress' approach (Section 6.4.2). The contribution of Q² analyses to model specification is examined in Section 6.5, with attention to the search for 'instruments' (section 6.5.1), the selection of variables and the uncovering of relationships (Section 6.5.2). Section 6.6 concludes.

6.1 Q² and the Causal Framework

In Section 4.1, an organizing framework was presented which situated Q² contributions in terms of a number of tasks and challenges posed in the

---

[1] A condensed version of parts of this chapter will appear as Shaffer (forthcoming).

identification stage of poverty analysis. For the causal stage of poverty analysis, a similar organizing framework is developed which directs attention to the contributions that Q² analyses have made to improving or broadening the causal framework. Specifically, such analyses have facilitated better, or fuller, identification of causal variables, weights, mechanisms, and the causal 'tree',[2] while also directing attention to issues of external validity.

Causal variables, as defined here, are events or facts which stand in a relationship of cause and effect to one another, that is the 'things' which do the causing or are caused. The causal tree, or diagram, represents the nature of the relationships among causal variables, and between causes and effects. Causal weights specify the relative importance of causes in producing effects. As discussed in Section 5.4, causal mechanisms provide explanations of 'how' and 'why' causes have the effects they do. In this discussion, we skirt debates and controversies surrounding the meaning of many of these terms which were addressed, in part, in Chapter 5. The objective here is simply to use these terms as a heuristic device to organize the Q² empirical studies.

In the Q² studies, this broadened causal framework has been used to analyse poverty status and poverty dynamics and to aid in model specification. Table 6.1 situates the key Q² empirical contributions in relation to these three areas of inquiry, namely, the determinants of poverty status and poverty dynamics, along with model specification, the four aspects of the causal framework, and external validity.

Table 6.1 Causal analysis: empirical contributions

	The causal framework				
	Variables	'Tree'	Weighting	Mechanism	External validity
Causal analysis					
The determinants of poverty					
i Combining outcomes and processes		x	x	x	x
ii The rural livelihood approach		x		x	
The determinants of poverty dynamics					
i Interviewing' the transition matrix	x	x	x	x	x
ii The stages of progress approach	x	x	x	x	
Model specification					
i Searching for 'instruments'	x		x		
ii Selecting variables and uncovering relationships	x	x	x	x	

x denotes that these issues are addressed (more or less successfully) by at least some of the empirical examples which fall under the headings.

[2] The terminology draws on Little (1998) and Schaffer (2008).

6.2 Distinguishing Poverty Status and Poverty Dynamics

Poverty dynamics is about the flow of households, or individuals, into and out of poverty and not simply the stock of poverty at one or more points in time.[3] Figure 6.1 elaborates upon this distinction between stocks and flow. It draws out certain of the core characteristics of these two concepts along with the related distinction between chronic and transitory poverty.

The notion of stocks of poverty is represented by circles on the left-hand side of the diagram, which represent the poor. In causal analysis of poverty status, these circles are undifferentiated, in that there is no distinction between the chronic and transitory poor. Analysis of determinants of poverty status may be conducted at a single point in time, as represented by the top circle, or over multiple time periods, as represented by both circles. It is a cross-sectional examination of the determinants of poverty. If conducted over time, analysis may address changes in the magnitude or characteristics of the stock of poverty along with their determinants.

Flows of poverty, on the other hand, involve tracking the same households, or individuals, over time. Such information facilitates the distinction between four categories of households, or individuals, namely those that

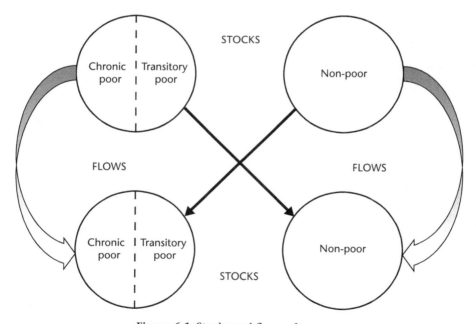

Figure 6.1 Stocks and flows of poverty

[3] This discussion draws on Shaffer (2008).

stay poor, escape from poverty, enter into poverty, or stay non-poor. The chronically poor represent the first of these categories while the 'transitorily' poor comprise the second and third categories.[4] In terms of Figure 6.1, chronic poverty comprises a portion of the 'poor' circle, shared with transitory poverty, as represented by those who have fallen into, or escaped, poverty. Such movements between categories of well-being are depicted by the arrows in the centre of the diagram. The policy relevance of this distinction is that different remedies may be appropriate for chronic and transitory poverty and for forms of transitory poverty, the latter two often associated with social protection policy and instruments (Barrientos and Hulme 2008).

In terms of Q², a further point concerns the rich variety of 'flows' or processes leading to entries or escapes from poverty. Figure 6.2 provides a more detailed depiction of such processes distinguishing between impoverishment, conjunctural, fluctuating poverty, and chronic poverty.

The first trajectory, chronic poverty, refers to the persistence of poverty over time. It represents a long-term or permanent condition, which differs from transitory forms of poverty. Chronic poverty may result from low levels of productivity in own agriculture, low real wages for labourers, and so forth.

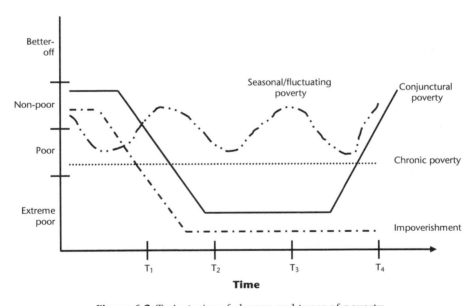

Figure 6.2 Trajectories of change and types of poverty

[4] Here, we are referring to the 'spells' approach to poverty dynamics rather than the 'components' approach (see Baulch and Hoddinott 2000). The latter defines chronic poverty as those whose average intertemporal income or consumption is less than the poverty line (Jalan and Ravallion 2000).

It may also concern the economically inactive who are unable to secure a livelihood due to disability or illness among other factors. Historically, most poverty reduction strategies have been designed to address this chronic dimension of poverty.

In terms of the dynamic trajectories of change depicted in Figure 6.2, impoverishment represents a dramatic fall in living conditions to a new long-term level. Six of the most prevalent precipitating factors of impoverishment in the Global South include illness, violence and conflict, natural disasters, harvest failure, terms of trade deterioration, and loss of employment (Sinha *et al.* 2002). Conjunctural poverty refers to increases in poverty due to circumstances which are likely to persist over the medium term. Examples include macroeconomic shocks, such as financial crises, the situation facing transition countries as well as major lifecycle changes. Fluctuating or seasonal poverty, or 'churning', refers to income variability in 'normal' times, such as over the course of an agricultural season, or following frequent and repeated natural shocks. As revealed in some of the empirical examples in this section, a major contribution of Q^2 analyses has been to unpack the notion of 'flows' by providing a rich account of the nature of the dynamic processes in question.

6.3 Determinants of Poverty Status

6.3.1 *Combining Outcomes and Processes*

> Economics is mainly about outcomes...[not] about processes. Economists, of course, have models of perfect competition, or bargaining to reach a Nash equilibrium, or surplus extraction and use by the dominant class. But economists' tests show only whether a modeled process is consistent with the measured outcomes...Only seldom does the economist empirically explore the processes themselves. (Lipton 1992: 1541)

As argued elsewhere (Bardhan and Ray 2006; Shaffer *et al.* 2008), a major contribution of Q^2 analysis has been to combine analyses of outcomes and processes. Historically, this is one of the main ways that 'qualitative' and 'quantitative' approaches have been integrated, with many good examples in the literature (e.g. Frankel and Lehmann 1984; Francis and Hoddinott 1993). Two such examples have been selected, both of which combine narrative information on processes with household survey results on outcomes.

In the early late 1990s and early 2000s, the International Food Policy Research Institute (IFPRI) conducted a study in rural Kenya on the effects of new agricultural technologies on the poor (Place *et al.* 2007). The technologies in question involved agro-forestry practices to replenish soil fertility.

Panel data were collected in 2000–1 from around 1,600 households on assets, expenditures, food consumption, technology use, and assorted household characteristics. At the same time, ethnographies were undertaken in a subset of forty households, over a six-month period by researchers who resided in the villages. The main methods used included participant observation, semi-structured interviews and, to a lesser extent, focus group discussions. The ethnographies provided detailed information on livelihoods, shocks, vulnerability, coping mechanisms, adaptations to technology, reasons for adoption of technology, and so forth.

The authors maintained that the Q² design significantly enriched research results in at least four ways. First, the household survey data facilitated the distinction between outlier and tendency cases with respect to both adoption and benefits of the new agricultural technology. For example, household survey data allowed for the statistical analysis of associations between poverty measures and the uptake of new technologies which could not have been undertaken using data from the ethnographies because of the small number of observations. In terms of the categories in the organizing framework, the Q² analysis facilitated the assessment of the external validity of the ethnographic results.

Second, the ethnographies helped interpret, and provided added additional information on, variables in the household survey. In terms of advantages or disadvantages of the new technologies, the survey response category 'too much labour required' conflated a number of distinct processes uncovered in the ethnographies. Specifically, issues arose concerning the gender distribution of labour, male migration, remittance income, and costs of hired labour, timing conflicts between new technologies and existing livelihood strategies, and so on. Further, the ethnographic information elaborated upon the multiple and variegated forms of modification and adoption of new technologies among villagers, which were presented in the household survey in terms of the fourfold categorization of 'never tried, dropped, testing, and adopted'. The Q² contribution, in this case, was to aid in the understanding of causal variables.

Third, the ethnographic data revealed varied reasons for the testing and adoption of new technology. The core assumption which informed the survey design was that income generation through higher maize yields constituted the primary objective underlying adoption. The ethnographies pointed to a range of ulterior motivations including selling seed to research and development organization and gaining access to social networks for perceived benefits at some later point. This example points to the role of Q² analysis in better explaining the causal mechanisms leading to observed outcomes.[5]

---

[5] Unpacking multiple sources of action, which offer differ from textbook utility or profit maximizing assumptions in applied micro-economics, is an area where ethnographic research has made important contributions (for example, Berry 1993; Mosse 2006).

Finally, the ethnographies allows for the explanation of certain counter-intuitive results from the household survey. For example, the analysis of household survey data did not find a statistically significant association between farm size and poverty. In the still relatively land abundant area of study, the core constraint on income generation, and poverty reduction, involved access to labour, not land.[6] Detailing the nature and extent of the labour constraint was a major contribution of the ethnographic results. The core Q^2 contribution in this instance was a better elaboration of the causal tree and causal mechanisms.

In terms of the organizing framework, the Q^2 design enhanced or facilitated the understanding of causal variables, mechanisms and the causal tree and allowed for an assessment of the external validity of the ethnographic results. It represents a high-quality attempt to draw on the respective strengths of a number of methodological approaches while recognizing their limitations.

The second example involves a study undertaken by Tassew Woldehanna and colleagues on child labour in Ethiopia as part of the *Young Lives* research project (Woldehanna *et al.* 2005, 2008). A household survey was implemented in 2002 and subsequent econometric work undertaken to estimate correlates of child schooling and labour. This analysis was followed-up by semi-structured interviews conducted in 2005 with a view to provide a richer understanding of the econometric results. A number of interesting findings emerged.

First, econometric results suggested, as expected, that the likelihood of children's participation in activities other than full-time schooling declines with paternal education. On the other hand, and surprisingly, the econometric analysis found the opposite result for maternal education. The semi-structured interviews provided an explanation. Women with higher levels of education are more likely to work outside their homes, which increases the domestic work burden of older children who assume responsibility for childcare and other tasks.

Second, regression results did not find a statistically significant effect of landholding size on the probability of children's schooling or participation in the labour market. Information from the semi-structured interviews suggested a number of explanations. First, children in households with more land are frequently working on the farm as would be expected given the high opportunity costs, or income foregone, of not working and imperfect labour or credit markets which precludes hiring sufficient labour. On the

---

[6] Iliffe (1987) has documented how the nature of poverty in sub-Saharan Africa changed gradually from lack of access to labour for purposes of farming to lack of access to land and/or inability to sell one's labour power.

other hand, children from households with less land are also frequently working, given the imperative of generating income in poorer families living at the margin. As a result, the 'opportunity cost effect' among households with large land size is offset by a 'wealth or poverty effect' among those with smaller landholdings, which renders insignificant the relationship between landholding and schooling.

Third, in the econometric analysis, an attempt was made to estimate the effect of caregiver social capital, measured in terms of variables such as the sense of trust, the number of community organizations that provide social support and so on. One interesting finding was the negative and statistically significant relationship between the number of social support organizations and the probability of child labour. This finding was counterintuitive, in that social support was expected to increase child schooling by diminishing the importance of the wealth or poverty effect, which compels children to work. A potential explanation from the semi-structured interviews was that social support often takes the form of food-for-work schemes in which children participate alongside their parents. Accordingly, the association between social capital and child labour was due to the nature of the social support provided.

In these examples, the key contribution of Q² has been to provide a more detailed account of likely causal mechanisms behind the observed outcomes, along with the interaction between variables, or the causal tree. It exemplifies the empirical application of 'conditional association' and 'mechanism-based approaches' to causation discussed in Chapter 5.

6.3.2 *The Rural Livelihoods Approach*

An example of a significant research programme which has used mixed methods to analyse the determinants of poverty, and rural livelihoods, is the Livelihoods and Diversification Directions Explored by Research (LADDER) programme led by the University of East Anglia's Frank Ellis. Studies were conducted in select sites in Uganda, Kenya, Tanzania, and Malawi in the early 2000s (Ellis and Freeman 2004).[7] The conceptual approach used for these studies was a version of the sustainable livelihoods framework (Scoones 1998), which has three main components.[8] First, the core causal variable consists of assets, or 'forms of capital', which are defined to include natural,

---

[7] The individual countries studies for Uganda, Tanzania, Malawi, and Kenya appear, respectively, as Ellis and Bahiigwa (2003), Ellis and Mdoe (2003), Ellis *et al.* (2003), and Freeman *et al.* (2004).

[8] Prior to the LADDER studies, Bebbington (1999) used a similar 'capitals and capabilities framework' to explain rural change in the Andes and Moser (1998) drew on a similar 'asset-vulnerability framework' to inform mixed method empirical studies in urban communities in Zambia, Ecuador, the Philippines, and Hungary.

physical, human, financial, and social dimensions of these terms. Next, a number of mediating processes are invoked which determine how forms of capital are used, by whom, and to what effect. Such mediating processes are related to social relations, institutions, organizations, shocks, and a number of longer term trends concerning population, migration, and technology, and so forth. Last, assets are transformed via these mediating forces into livelihood strategies which comprise both natural resource and non-natural resource-based activities. These three components are succinctly summarized in Ellis' definition of a livelihood:

> a livelihood comprises the assets (natural, physical, human, financial and social capital), the activities and the access to these (mediated by institutions and social relations) that together determine the living gained by the individual or household. (Ellis 2000: 10)

Methodologically, the studies combined fixed response household survey questionnaires with Participatory Rural Appraisal (PRA) techniques including, wealth ranking, focus group discussions, institutional mapping, calendars, and time lines. Household survey data provided information on assets, incomes, shocks, and livelihood activities, which corresponds broadly to the first and third components of the sustainable livelihood framework, namely assets and livelihood strategies. Information from the PRAs placed emphasis on the second component, mediating processes, related primarily to institutions, though also enriching the analysis of livelihood strategies. The use of mixed methods served to present a richer causal analysis and strengthen the causal claims made.

For example, one finding from the household survey data in all four countries concerns the close association of asset ownership, in particular land and livestock, and income levels (Ellis and Freeman 2004:11–12). While bivariate associations of this type are suggestive of causal relations, they are not conclusive for reasons related to third factors and reverse causation, among others, discussed in Section 5.2. In the individual case studies, the causal claim was greatly strengthened by narrative information from the focus groups which outlined the processes behind the associated outcomes. In Uganda, for example (Ellis and Bahiigwa 2003: 1004):

> the picture that emerges [from the mixed methods] is that one or two key assets, for example education land or livestock, can provide the lead into a successful accumulation path. The poor are characterized by their inability to get an initial purchase on this upward process or by the occurrence of personal crises in which previous assets have been depleted to below the critical starting point.

Another key finding from the household surveys concerned the importance of non-farm income (wages, self-employment and remittances) to poverty reduction. In all four countries, the importance of agricultural income declines as household income rises (Ellis and Freeman 2004: 17). A core contribution of the narrative information was to explain certain of the mediating processes which preclude such diversification among the poor. A number of institutional barriers were identified including payoffs to traditional leaders, burdensome licensing requirements, onerous taxes on crops and livestock and other official and unofficial roadblocks. The narrative information helped explain the causal mechanisms which lay behind the observed outcomes.

Overall, the mixed method approach allowed for a stronger and richer causal picture to emerge by combining data on outcomes with information on the causal mechanisms and the causal tree. As such, it presented an applied example of conditional association and mechanism-based approaches to causation discussed in Chapter 5. Arguably, however, there was scope to deepen the methodological integration from one based on different research teams independently addressing separate questions within the sustainable livelihoods framework.[9] For example, findings from the PRA exercises were used to construct the sampling frame for the household survey, but not apparently, to develop the questionnaire. Certain of the findings on obstacles to diversification could have been included in the household survey which in principle, would have allowed subsequent analysis to assess their prevalence and relative importance (as in the Stages of Progress studies discussed in Section 6.4). Nevertheless, the Q² approach added value over either the household survey, or the PRA, conducted on its own.

6.4 Determinants of Poverty Dynamics

As discussed in Section 6.2, poverty dynamics concerns the flows of households into and out of poverty and not simply the stocks of poverty. Analysis of flows allows one to distinguish between those who remain poor, escape from poverty, enter into poverty and remain non-poor. This basic categorization can be depicted in terms of a 2 × 2 poverty transition matrix which represents the flows of poor and non-poor households at two points of time. All of the Q² studies discussed in this section have added value to the causal analysis of poverty dynamics by providing a fuller explanation, and better understanding, of this transition matrix.[10]

---

[9] The sustainable livelihoods framework itself has been critiqued for, *inter alia*, its inadequate treatment of a range of issues including, global or macro-level phenomena, power, class, politics, and long-term shifts in climate and rural economies (see O'Laughlin 2004; Scoones 2009).

[10] There is an older tradition in applied social anthropology and 'anthropological' economics, which is not discussed, of undertaking 'qualitative panels' based on longitudinal ethnographic

6.4.1 'Interviewing' the Transition Matrix

A number of recent studies have combined panel data from household surveys with detailed studies of households who fall within different quadrants of the poverty transition matrix.[11] Typically, the objective has been to supplement descriptive statistical or regression results from the panel data with a more detailed understanding of the processes generating outcomes. In terms of the above terminology, causal weighting is combined with a deeper understanding of causal variables, mechanisms, and the causal tree.

The first such example is the study by Barrett *et al.* (2006) on welfare dynamics in rural Kenya and Madagascar as part of USAID's BASIS Collaborative Research Support Program. The study applies the analytical and methodological framework of Carter and Barrett (2006) to determine if poverty traps exist. The approach distinguishes between the structural component of poverty, estimated based on asset holdings and return on assets, and its stochastic component due to chance. In the present study, the authors searched for the existence of asset poverty traps, or thresholds below which households are unable to accumulate enough assets, or increase returns on existing assets, to escape poverty. The existence of such traps implies increasing returns to assets at some point as one moves along the income/consumption distribution as richer households have access to higher earning opportunities than poorer households.

The econometric component of the methodology drew on panel datasets, of various intervals, from northern and western Kenya and Madagascar. It entailed, first, estimating expected structural income change as a function of asset holdings and, next, regressing expected structural income against beginning period income. If poverty traps exist, one would expect to see declining expected income for lower income groups which subsequently reverses as increasing returns set in. Non-parametric regression results do, in fact, reveal such a pattern.

The key contribution of the 'qualitative' component of the study was to explain why such a pattern emerges. Detailed case studies were conducted of select households who were situated within different categories of the poverty transition matrix. Oral histories were undertaken to uncover the reasons behind the well-being trajectories of particular households. Such information revealed at least three processes which were consistent with the above finding of increasing local returns to assets.

First, capital constraints precluded the poor from meeting start-up costs associated with higher return activities such as zero grazing dairy production

studies which often integrated numerical and narrative information. Examples include Haswell (1975), Hill (1977), Lanjouw and Stern (1998), Whitehead (2002, 2006), and Epstein (2007).
[11] Similar studies which are not discussed here include Little *et al.* (2006) and Lawson *et al.* (2008).

with cross-bred cows and commercial tea cultivation. Second, the lack of education and higher level connections served as barriers to more remunerative employment, such as salaried jobs in the public or private sectors. Third, the fear of asset loss, due to various shocks, relegate many poor cultivators to low-risk/low-return activities,[12] a fact confirmed by subsequent econometric analysis of the panel data.

In terms of the above terminology, the Q² analysis allowed for the combination of causal weights and mechanisms with a more detailed account of the causal tree. The study is a high-quality example of the applied use of conditional association and mechanism-based approaches to causation. The oral histories served to bring alive, and bolster the validity of, the econometric evidence in support of poverty traps.

A second high-quality example involves Baulch and Davis' (2008) study in Bangladesh conducted under the auspices of the Chronic Poverty Research Centre. This study combined three waves of panel data, between 1996 and 2003, with life histories of around 300 individuals conducted in 2006–7. The individuals selected for the life histories were in different quadrants in the estimated poverty transition matrices. The panel data allowed for the presentation of descriptive statistics on poverty transitions along with subsequent econometric analysis on determinants of poverty transitions and consumption expenditure per capita (Quisumbing 2011). The life histories provided a much richer depiction of the nature of trajectories of change.

Four patterns of change emerged from the narrative information, described as 'smooth, saw-tooth, single step, and multi-step processes', which are either upward or downward trending. Of these, the vast majority (146 of 184 cases) were characterized by the saw-tooth pattern in which improvements and declines follow one another intermittently. Positive changes related to business income, land, livestock, and employment trigger gradual improvements which are often suddenly reversed by negative shocks associated with illness or injury, dowry/marriage, death of a family member, and so forth. The frequency of such events and their varied nature make them hard to capture in standard panel household surveys. In addition, the non-linear nature of the processes in question may be incorrectly specified in econometric models which restrict the functional form of such relationships in various ways.

Overall, the Q² analysis allowed for the combination of causal weights from the econometric analysis with a rich depiction of causal mechanisms and the causal tree from the life histories. Accordingly, it represents the combined use of approaches to causation based on conditional association and mechanisms. The detailed description of well-being trajectories serves to elaborate upon the processes underlying the dynamics of poverty in Figure 6.2.

---

[12] Wood (2003) has characterized the low risk/low return option as the 'Faustian' bargain.

Additional benefits of the mixed method approach for model specification are discussed in Section 6.5.2.

A final example of this genre of research is a collaborative study conducted in KwaZulu-Natal, South Africa, by the University of Natal, the International Food Policy Research Institute (IFPRI), the University of Wisconsin-Madison, and the Catholic University of Peru (Adato *et al.* 2006, 2007). The study employed a very similar methodology as that of Barrett *et al.* (2006). Two waves of panel data (1993 and 1998) from the KwaZulu Natal Income Dynamics Survey (KIDS) were combined with detailed case studies of households located at different quadrants in the poverty transition matrices. As with Barrett *et al.* (2006) the econometric analysis found evidence of poverty traps for those households below a critical asset threshold.

The core contribution of the case studies, conducted in 2001, was to probe in greater detail the experiences of different household types with emphasis on the events precipitating downward and upward well-being trajectories. One of the key findings to emerge involved the role of social capital, which was not included among assets used to estimate structural income in the econometric analysis.[13] The term itself was found to mask around twenty different ways in which social assets are used, including assistance in looking for work, burial societies, cash, rotating savings and credit associations, community gardens, etc.

Assistance in finding employment was considered of central importance though often unsuccessful given high rates of unemployment. This finding provides support for the underlying thesis that structural poverty 'matters'. Specifically, social capital was not found to be a viable pathway out of poverty in the absence of access to productive assets or employment.

In terms of Table 6.1, the Q^2 analysis allowed for a better understanding of causal variables, causal mechanisms, and the causal tree. It improved the explanation of drivers of change, how they interact, and why. It also represents the combined use of approaches to causation based on conditional association and mechanisms.

6.4.2 *The 'Stages of Progress' approach*

The Stages of Progress (SoP) approach[14] was developed by Duke University's Anirudh Krishna in 2002 and has been applied to over 35,000 households

---

[13] It was included, however, in other modelling work using the same dataset (Maluccio *et al.* 2000).

[14] A similar methodology, entitled the 'Ladder of Life' approach, was used in the World Bank's *Moving out of Poverty* studies. The methodology was introduced in Volume 2 (Narayan *et al.* 2009) and combined with forms of econometric analysis in Volume 3 on India (Narayan 2009). We focus on the SoP approach which preceded it.

in India, Kenya, Uganda, Peru, and North Carolina. Results of these studies have led to numerous publications, recently summarized in Krishna (2010a,b). I focus on those studies which combined information on people's perceptions about reasons for escapes from, or descents into, poverty with various forms of statistical analysis. First, the methodology is outlined in brief.

The SoP methodology contains four stages relevant to the analysis of the dynamics of poverty. First, local understandings of poverty are elicited by asking communities to identify what households do, in sequence, when they emerge gradually from a state of acute poverty, or through which 'stages of progress' do they pass. Second, a poverty line is drawn based on local understandings of the stages associated with poverty and prosperity. Third, drawing on recall data, households are classified into one of four categories in the poverty transition matrix based on their poverty status in the past and present. Fourth, reasons for escape from, and descents into, poverty of particular households are elicited from focus groups and specific households. The first two steps concern the poverty identification stage discussed in Section 3,[15] while the last two concern causal analysis.

The selection of causal variables is based on people's perceptions of reasons for descents and escapes. In fact, the causal claim is based on local knowledge of the processes which have led to changes in one's poverty status. Such information allows for the compilation of lists of principle reasons for escapes and entries based on the percentage of households which identified them. Accordingly, poor health and health-related expenses were found to be the main reasons for descents into poverty across all studies conducted in the Global South. These factors were the principal reasons cited for between 60% and 88% of descents (Krishna 2010b: 79). The core contribution of the analysis, at this point, was to provide a fuller account of causal variables along with an understanding of how they effect change. As such, it is an example of a mechanism-based approached to causation.

The next stage in the SoP analysis involves modelling 'reasons', with a view to provide information on causal weights. In Uganda and Peru, logistic (logit) regression models were estimated of the likelihood of falling into, or escaping, poverty (Krishna *et al.* 2006a,b). The relative importance of variables, conditional on all others, is inferred by comparing the size of logit coefficients or odds ratios.[16]

---

[15] The SoP methodology is unlikely to satisfy requirements of 'basket' and 'levels' consistency required for consistent interpersonal comparisons, discussed in Chapter 4. With respect to basket consistency, however, there was a remarkable degree of homogeneity across all sites concerning the initial stages of progress associated with food, clothing, and shelter/home repairs.

[16] The latter provide a more intuitive understanding of coefficient values in terms of probabilities.

A variant of this approach, in Gujarat, India, entailed exploration of 'net events', which is simply the difference between the number of positive and negative events experienced by a household (Krishna and Lecy 2008). Visual inspection of the relationship between net events and change in poverty status reveal a sigmoid ('S-shaped') pattern with a diminishing (but positive) effect of the number of events above three and below negative two. Subsequent regression analysis found that this 'net event' variable remains significant even when conditioning on various types of individual events experienced by households. In addition, a technique known as association discovery, or market basket analysis, was used to identify events commonly grouped together, which entered the model as interaction terms.

Overall, the Q^2 analysis of SoP approach allowed for a rich depiction of causal variables, mechanisms, and the causal tree to be combined with causal weighting facilitated by econometric analysis. The causal claim is based on people's perceptions of underlying mechanisms but econometric results are used to assess the validity of the alleged causal variables, by reviewing their statistical significance, and to gauge their relative importance. Accordingly, it is an example of the integrated use of mechanism-based and 'conditional association' approaches to causation.

The main methodological concerns involve the heavy reliance on recall to infer well-being trajectories, which may be subject to various biases as discussed in Section 3.3, and the relatively short duration of community stays, one to two days, which may account for the homogeneity of results about dimensions of poverty, mentioned in note 15 of this chapter.

6.5 Model Specification

The preceding sections have addressed specific ways that Q^2 approaches have facilitated causal analysis of poverty status and poverty dynamics. Here, examples are presented of how various types of narrative information have proved useful for purposes of econometric modelling more generally.

6.5.1 *Searching for 'Instruments'*

A first example illustrates the so-called 'participatory econometrics' approach pursued by Vijayendra Rao of the World Bank (Rao 2002, 2003). In their study of sex workers in Calcutta, Rao *et al.* (2003) sought to estimate the revenue loss, or compensating differential, associated with condom use. The main econometric problem is that unobserved characteristics of sex workers, which are correlated *both* with condom use and prices, can bias results. For example, if sex workers with more desirable, but unobserved attributes, are better able to require condom use of clients *and* to command high prices, then there will be a downward bias in the value of the differential.

The key Q² contribution was to use dialogical techniques to search for an instrumental variable, or instrument, to deal with the econometric problem. When attempting to estimate the causal effect of x on y, an instrument is a third variable which affects y only through its effect on x. In this case, it must affect the price of sex acts only through its effect on condom use, and not be correlated with unobserved variables which also affect prices. Through semi-structured interviews, the research uncovered just such an instrument. The All India Institute of Public Health and Hygiene has initiated an HIV/ AIDs awareness programme throughout the area which was implemented in a seemingly random manner. Further, participation in the programme appeared to be effective at promoting condom use. Accordingly, participation in this programme was used as an instrument to estimate the relationship between condom use and price. In terms of the terminology of Table 6.1, Q² facilitated the identification of causal variables for modelling purposes.

6.5.2 *Selecting Variables and Uncovering Relationships*

A second example is de Weerdt's (2010) study of poverty transitions in Kagera, Tanzania, which was undertaken as part of the World Bank's *Moving out of Poverty* study. The study drew on the Kagera Health and Development Survey (KHDS) which collected panel data in 1994 and 2004 along with focus group discussions and life histories. Econometric analysis was performed on the data with a view to predict 2004 asset values on the basis of 1993 household characteristics. A comparison of model predictions with actual 2004 data revealed significant discrepancies. In particular, only around half of those whose asset values were predicted to increase actually did so. The key role of the Q² analysis, was to use dialogical methods to explain why certain households had 'defied their economic destiny'.

The narrative information suggested a number of factors as explanations of deviations from predictions of the model. Concerning 'unexpected losers', one explanation concerned intervening events between waves of the panel such as agricultural shocks, mortality, illness, and widowhood or death. A second reason for the discrepancies had to do with variables not included in the survey such as alcoholism, bad marital relations, and lack of exposure to outside information. With respect to 'surprise winners', missing variables in the survey, such as exposure to outside ideas and networks, were important as was the incorrect specification of the causal structure of the model, in particular the interaction between remoteness and initial conditions.

The life histories and focus groups suggested reasons why the interaction between initial conditions and remoteness, and not only their individual effects, was important by contrasting the situation in remote and non-remote villages. In the latter, initial conditions proved less important due to opportunities associated with trade, such as the availability of employment as casual labourers, the emergence of business relationships with outside traders, and the influx of money and access to new ideas and networks outside the village. These positive effects were absent in remote villages which compounded the effects of poor initial conditions. In light of these findings, a respecified model was estimated including an interaction term of remoteness and initial conditions which proved to be statistically significant. In terms of Table 6.1, the contribution of Q^2 was to aid in the specification of causal variables and their interrelationships, or the causal tree, along with an understanding of the underlying causal mechanisms at work.

A final example concerns the econometric estimation of panel data from the Chronic Poverty Research Centre's study on Bangladesh discussed in Section 6.4.1. This study included an initial stage of focus group discussions to refine research questions and identify variables for inclusion in the household survey. A second stage combined panel data with life histories. The contribution of Q^2 to variable and model specification is aptly described by Agnes Quisumbing, who conducted the econometric work:

> Nesting a quantitative analysis of poverty dynamics within a fully-integrated qualitative and quantitative study has also yielded insights that might not have been possible with one approach alone. The focus group discussions, conducted prior to the fielding of the quantitative survey, brought out specific issues that were addressed through the design or adaptation of specialized questionnaire modules, such as those focusing on shocks. While the shocks module was similar to those administered in other countries, its adaptation to the Bangladesh context—particularly the disaggregation of illness shocks into income losses and medical expenses—was reinforced by the focus group discussions. The life histories work identified the severe deleterious effects of combined dowry and illness expenses as an important factor that put households on a downward life trajectory. This led to the re-specification of the shocks variables to include these combined shocks, which have been found to reduce the probability of moving out of poverty. (Quisumbing 2011: 54)

In terms of Table 6.1, the Q^2 approach has allowed for a better specification of causal variables and an improved understanding of causal mechanisms and the causal tree. Once again, it represents the integration of 'conditional association' and 'mechanism-based' approaches to causation.

6.6 Conclusion

The causal stage of poverty analysis asks 'Why are people poor?'. Chapter 5 made a theoretical case for causal pluralism by arguing that there are a range of different conceptions of causation, and associated models of causal inference, which are relevant, in principle, to answering this question. This chapter has assessed the empirical case for causal pluralism by examining whether or not such approaches succeed in practice. Overall, the empirical case is strong. Examples of value-added abound.

Specifically, it was argued that Q^2 studies have added value by improving, and/or broadening, analysis of four aspects of the causal framework, namely causal variables, weights, mechanisms, and the causal 'tree', while also directing attention to issues of external validity. In terms of causal analysis of poverty status, empirical examples were presented where analyses of outcomes and processes were fruitfully integrated, including a series of studies which used the rural livelihoods framework. Such examples illustrate the applied use of conditional association and mechanism-based approaches to causation.

With respect to causal analysis of poverty dynamics, studies were presented which combined analysis of panel data from household surveys with detailed interviews of households in different cells of the poverty transition matrix which provided a richer and more accurate analysis of the causal framework. A further example of such valued added was provided through a review of studies using the Stages of Progress approach. Finally, the contribution of Q^2 analysis to model specification was illustrated by examining a number of studies which used mixed methods to facilitate the search for instrumental variables, the selection of variables and the understanding of the nature of their interrelationships.

Q^2 research designs add value to the analysis of poverty status and poverty dynamics. Do they yield similar benefits when assessing the impact of development programmes or projects? This question is the subject of Chapter 7.

Chapter 7

Q² Impact Assessment: Evaluating the Poverty Impact of Programmes and Projects

Chapter 6 presented a range of examples of causal analysis of poverty in the Q² tradition, distinguishing between analyses of poverty status and poverty dynamics. This chapter addresses a second area where Q² techniques have been applied to causal analysis, namely impact assessment. Whereas causal analysis of poverty asks the question 'Why are people poor?', impact assessment asks 'Who benefits, how much, and why?' from development programmes or projects. Causation is deeply implicated in answering these questions.

Following an opening section which defines impact assessment and reviews methods (Section 7.1), this chapter is structured around four core contributions that Q² analyses have made to assessing the impact of development programmes and projects. Specifically, such analyses have facilitated integrated analysis of mechanisms and results (Section 7.2), and comparison group construction (Section 7.3), allowed for alternative ways of constructing counterfactuals such as thought experiments (Section 7.4) and directed attention to the question of the valuation of different programme benefits by participants (Section 7.5). A final section concludes.

The issues addressed in this chapter were chosen to illustrate the contributions of Q² to impact assessment. The focus is on impact assessment of programmes or projects not policies. In terms of the discussion in Chapter 5, emphasis is placed on the counterfactual dependence and mechanism-based conceptions of causation, along with their attendant models of causal inference. There are other approaches to impact evaluation, such as partial and general equilibrium analyses, which address multi-sector or economy-wide impacts of policies (Bourguignon and da Silva 2003), which are not addressed. Also, there is limited consideration of the role of mixed methods in programme monitoring and evaluation (Rallis and Rossman 2003), which differs from impact assessment in a number of ways.[1]

---

[1] Other surveys with additional examples include Rao and Woolcock (2003), White (2008), and Bamberger *et al.* (2010).

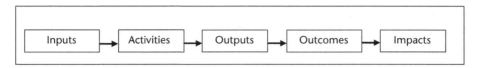

Figure 7.1 The impact chain

7.1 Definitions and Methods

There is no consensus definition of impact assessment and it consequently ends up referring to different things (White 2009a).[2] For the present purposes, impact assessment is defined in terms of two core characteristics:

i. it is concerned with outcomes or impacts and not programme inputs, activities or outputs;

ii. it attempts to 'attribute' outcomes or impacts to specific programmes, and does not simply track changes in them and as such, uses techniques to address the so-called 'attribution' problem.

The input-impact terminology draws on the concept of the impact chain presented in Figure 7.1 (Roche 1999). The impact chain depicts the causal relationships in programmes or projects from inputs through activities and outputs, culminating in outcomes or impacts. Inputs refer to the financial, physical and human resource requirements for the implementation of project activities. Activities are the tasks undertaken to realize programme objectives. Outputs are the goods or services resulting directly from the successful implementation of activities. Outcomes and impacts reflect longer term project effects usually on some dimension of well-being. While these distinctions tend to blur in practice, the key point is that impact assessment tends to focus on the right-hand side of Figure 7.1, whereas standard project monitoring and evaluation on the left-hand side.

The second defining characteristic of impact assessment, addressing the attribution problem, stems from the fact that most outcome and impact indicators are affected by many variables which have nothing to do with a particular development project or programme. One of the features of impact assessment is its attempt to control for the effects of these other 'confounding variables' when assessing the impact of a project of programme. Otherwise stated, impact assessment attempts to make a *causal link* between the project or programme under investigation and the outcome or impact variables of interest. This causal claim is the second distinguishing characteristic of impact assessment.

---

[2] This discussion is based on Shaffer (2011).

Of the different ways to establish a causal link, this chapter focuses on those which are based on counterfactual dependence and mechanism-based conceptions of causation and models of causal inference, discussed in Sections 5.3 and 5.4, respectively. In the context of impact assessment, counterfactual analyses involve either experimental or quasi-experimental approaches. For the former, programme participation is randomly assigned and consequently, population characteristics of treatment and controls groups are identical in expectation over large enough numbers (Duflo *et al.* 2008). The main complicating factors arise when assumptions of the underlying model are violated. Examples include incomplete compliance with assignment, externalities or spill-overs between treatment and control groups, non-random attrition among treatment and controls, and so forth. There is a large literature on how to address these applied problems which usually involves using econometric models to adjust for them in a number of ways (Duflo *et al.* 2008).

There is a much wider variety of quasi-experimental approaches to impact assessment which differ in the statistical techniques used to construct comparison groups. Some of the better known approaches include regression discontinuity designs, where individual just above and just below project eligibility thresholds are compared, pipeline approaches where eligible persons in line for project participation are compared with actual project participants, and matching procedures whereby individuals in comparison and treatment groups are matched on the basis of similar observable characteristics (Ravallion 2008). One widely used technique, propensity score matching, uses logistic regressions to estimate the probability of participation, or the propensity score, which serves as the basis for the subsequent matching, though other non-parametric matching estimators are also available (Abadie and Imbens 2009). In both experiments and quasi-experiments, the estimate of project impact, or the average treatment effect on the treated, is the difference in value of outcome indicators between treatment and control groups.

Applied mechanism-based approaches attempt to forge causal links between programme activities or outputs and development outcomes or impacts, drawing on theory or the results of dialogic inquiry. Examples of such approaches include the Context–Mechanism–Outcome (CMO) model of Realistic Evaluation (Pawson and Tilley 1997; Pawson 2002), applied instances of theory-based evaluation (Weiss 2000; White 2009b), some types of participatory assessment (Mayoux and Chambers 2005) applied ethnographic evaluations (Adato 2008), process-tracing designs (George and Bennett 2004), and others. Most of the examples presented in this chapter rely heavily on dialogical methods, such as focus group discussions and semi-structured interviews, to establish the causal links in question, though participant observation is also used.

7.2 Combining Results and Mechanisms

A core contribution of Q² approaches in impact assessment has been to combine analyses of programme outcomes and impacts, or 'results', with an examination of the underlying mechanisms generating them. As such, it represents an applied example of the combination of counterfactual dependence and mechanism-based approaches to causation. Further, it is the corollary in the context of impact assessment, of combining outcomes and process in causal analysis of poverty, discussed in Chapter 6.

There are many good examples in the literature of the combined analysis of results and mechanisms using a range of analytical techniques. Two such studies were undertaken by the International Food Policy Research Institute (IFPRI) in Nicaragua and Turkey to assess the impact of conditional cash transfer (CCT) schemes (Adato 2008). Both of these impact evaluations integrated experimental or quasi-experimental designs with ethnographic studies to provide a combined account of results and mechanisms.

The Nicaraguan CCT programme, the *Red de Protección Social* (RPS) provided cash and in-kind benefits to participants on condition that they attend health and nutrition workshops and their children participate in growth monitoring and vaccination programmes. Children also received nutritional supplements, including iron, and anti-parasite treatments.

The experimental component of the impact assessment drew on the fact that programme placement was random. Specifically, twenty-one of forty-two poor[3] administrative areas (*comarcas*) in the northern part of the Central Region were randomly selected for programme participation. Household surveys, with a range of modules on social outcomes indicators, were administered in 2000, prior to the start of the programme, and again in 2002. Accordingly, programme impact was measured as the 'double-difference' between programme participants and non-participants between 2000 and 2002. The ethnographic component involved village stays of four to five months and entailed multiple household visits by field researchers who conducted semi-structured interviews and engaged in participant observation.

One striking finding from the experimental analysis was the absence of any programme impact on anaemia, despite a sharp rise in the percentage of children receiving iron supplements. The double difference analysis found a slightly negative, but not statistically significant, programme impact despite the increase, from 24% to 80%, in the percentage of children receiving iron supplements. The ethnographic study provided a potential explanation. Despite respondent claims in semi-structured interviews that they were

---

[3] These forty-two *comarcas* were selected on the basis of a set of poverty indicators including access to potable water, latrines and illiteracy rates (Maluccio and Flores 2005: 4–5).

providing iron supplements, only three of sixty case study households were observed to be doing so.[4] The narrative information attributed this apparent reluctance to the bad taste of iron and adverse side-effects including vomiting and diarrhoea (Adato 2008: 229). In this case, information from the ethnographies provided a potential explanation for lack of programme impact uncovered through the experimental analysis.

The second IFPRI impact evaluation was conducted on Turkey's Social Risk Mitigation Programme, which became fully operational in 2004. The programme provided cash payments conditional on school enrolment for boys and girls along with vaccinations and regular check-ups for children. As above, ethnographic work in six localities was combined with a quasi-experimental analysis drawing on household survey data. The particular technique used, regression discontinuity design, compares outcomes among households who fell just above, and just below, the eligibility threshold for programme participation.

The quasi-experimental analysis found that the programme raised secondary school enrolment for girls by around 10%, a statistically significant effect. Nevertheless, secondary enrolment rates remained low for programme participants in rural areas. For example, secondary enrolment rates for girls were below 40%. The key contribution of the ethnographic work was to explain some of the reasons why. For boys, doubts were expressed about the value of education in the context of high unemployment and a society where honour is bestowed on those working on the land. For girls, the potential employment or wage effect of additional schooling was not highly valued given the overriding importance of their traditional female roles as mothers and wives. Further, concerns were raised about threats to family honour and reputation associated with girls' schooling. According to one father in a village in the province of Van: 'the girls have only their honour as a valuable thing in the village and it is my duty to prevent any bad words about that...No one sends their daughters to school anyway. Why should I send mine? They will look at them in a bad way' (Adato 2008: 231). As above, the core contribution of the ethnographic work was to provide an account of the mechanisms generating the somewhat disappointing results about programme impact.

A final example of combining mechanisms and results involves a mixed methods impact assessment of the Transport Sector Support Program (PAST) rural infrastructure project in Nicaragua (Broegaard *et al.* 2011). In one area covered by this study, Las Segovias, narrative information from focus group

---

[4] This example illustrates the use of observation, not simply dialogue, in ethnographic inquiry and highlights differences between applied social anthropology and PRA techniques discussed in Section 2.1.

discussions and semi-structured interviews was combined with results of a double difference quasi-experimental design involving propensity score matching. The data source for the latter included a baseline survey carried out in 2001 along with a resurvey undertaken in the context of the impact assessment.

One important finding from the double difference analysis was that the programme had a positive and statistically significant effect on employment in both agriculture and construction. It was estimated that the project increased the number of hours worked per week by between 9.5 and 12.3 hours (Rand 2010). The narrative information corroborated this finding and identified a number of the underlying reasons.

In the construction sector, there was a learning effect from the PAST projects in that other municipalities increasingly adopted similar labour-intensive methods. Further, past project participants gained employment due, in part, to their construction experience with PAST. With respect to agriculture, the employment boost was attributed to changes in relative prices between inputs and outputs and the attendant modifications to incentives. More specifically, employment was generated through the following processes: (i) prices received by farmers rose due to more frequent, timelier, and less expensive contacts with buyers; (ii) revenue increased through reduction in post-harvest losses of higher value, perishable products; (iii) land area under cultivation rose, increasing demand for on-farm employment. The narrative results provided evidence on the mechanisms generating results and provided empirical support for the validity of the quasi-experimental findings.

7.3 Identifying Comparison Groups

As discussed in Section 7.1, applied examples of counterfactual dependence are predicated on the use of a control or comparison group of programme non-participants. A core issue for quasi-experimental approaches, however, concerns unobservable population characteristics which may be affecting programme participation and outcomes. If the distribution of such characteristics differs between treatment and comparison groups, then impact results may be biased either positively or negatively. A core argument in favour of randomization is that it minimizes this 'selection bias' in that characteristics of treatment and comparison groups are equal in expectation over large enough numbers (Duflo *et al.* 2008).

One contribution of Q² analysis has been to draw on a wider range of sources of information to address the problem of selection bias. A hypothetical example is provided in Martin Ravallion's (2001) fictional account of a chance encounter between 'Ms. Analyst' and 'Ms. Sensible Sociologist'. The former is on a quest to find ways to address selection bias in her quasi-experimental impact assessment of an education project. A chance encounter with Ms Sensible Sociologist reveals information on the determinants of programme participation, namely that is heavily influenced by the school board in which one happens to live. Since all school boards receive the same allocation, a poor household living in a better-off school board has a higher chance of participation. Accordingly, a variable representing budget allocation to school boards could be used to estimate a model of participation, such as propensity score matching, which subsequently can be used as an instrumental variable in a model of schooling. In this case, narrative information on the determinants of programme participation uncovered an observable variable which could be used in subsequent modelling.

In addition to uncovering observable variables, attempts have been made to incorporate either unmeasured or unobserved information for use in the construction of comparison groups. An example is provided in Rao and Ibáñez's (2005) impact assessment of the Jamaica Social Investment Fund (JSIF), which financed a range of small scale projects proposed by local communities. In the impact assessment, detailed dialogic inquiry, including focus group discussions and semi-structured interviews, preceded the administration of a household survey and subsequent propensity score matching analysis.

Five communities were chosen for the impact assessment. The first stage in comparison group construction was to pair these communities with five other similar ones. This pairing exercise first took into account poverty scores used by the JSIF drawing on census data. Focus group discussions were then held to narrow down the pool of potential pairs, incorporating unmeasured variables such as geography, occupational structure, number of churches, youth groups, and so forth. Field visits were also conducted to improve the match, by taking into account 'unobservables' such as political culture and social structure.

The second stage consisted of data collection for the propensity score matching. Here, a number of contextual variables were including in the household survey on the basis of the previously collected narrative information such as Rastafarian affiliation and the availability of social networks. Overall, the authors maintained that use of these additional sources of information contributed to minimizing the problem of selection bias (Rao and Ibáñez 2005: 81). Unfortunately, it was not possible, within the design of this study, to test if the 'improved' comparison group mattered for impact results by examining, for example, if results were sensitive to the choice of comparison groups.

7.4 Conducting Counterfactual Thought Experiments

In addition to providing information on unobservable or unmeasured variables, Q² approaches have contributed to comparison group construction through the use of thought experiments or mental simulation exercises. An example was provided in the 2003–4 impact assessment of the national Hunger Eradication and Poverty Reduction (HEPR) in Vietnam[5]. The HEPR programme comprised a number of targeted projects as well as policies on health care, education, and social support for the poor. The impact assessment was innovative in that it attempted to combine two ways of constructing a comparison groups with a view to determine if they would generate similar results or, if not, to spur reflection as to why.

The first approach involved propensity score matching. The primary objective of this exercise was to conduct sensitivity analysis on the results of a similar, prior analysis conducted by the World Bank in 2003.[6] Specifically, it assessed the sensitivity of results of the World Bank analysis to the choice of comparison group by presenting results for the nearest one, three and five matched non-beneficiaries. In addition, standard errors were calculated and confidence intervals presented for the impact estimates. The data source for the analysis was the Vietnam Household Living Standard Survey 2002 (VHLSS), a multi-topic nationally representative survey, which contained a module on participation in specific HEPR projects.

The second approach used in the HEPR study relied on a thought experiment, rather than intersubjectively observable information, to arrive at an appropriate counterfactual. As discussed in Section 5.3, intersubjective observability is quite integral to the Holland–Rubin framework which defines the problem of causal inference as a problem of observation. Subjunctive conditional (if–then) questions were posed about what respondents would have done in the absence of the programme.

In order to get meaningful answers to questions of this type, a mental simulation exercise is required which faces potential biases relating to human judgement (Elster 1987; Gilovich and Griffin 2002), survey design (Sudman *et al.* 1996), and the nature of dialogic processes (Chambers 2003b). Further, meaningful responses become increasingly difficult the greater the causal distance between programme activities and the outcome/impact variable, the greater the number of intervening variables affecting outcomes/impacts, the more complex the pattern of interaction among variables and the finer the scale in which the outcome/impact variable is measured (e.g. cardinal vs. ordinal). Nevertheless, it is worthwhile to examine whether such perceptual information

---

[5] This section is based on Shaffer (2012).
[6] Results were published in the JDR (2004) and appear in Cuong (n.d.).

differs systematically from intersubjective observables in the HEPR study. In the HEPR impact assessment, the two approaches were used for two project components: the Health Fee Reduction or Exemption programme, which assessed utilization of health services and the Tuition and School Maintenance Fee Exemption or Reduction which assessed primary and secondary enrolment.

The Health Fee Exemption or Reduction entailed providing poor households or communes free or subsidised health care through (i) the distribution of health insurance cards or poor household certificates which entitle the holders to free or subsided care; and (ii) the direct provision of free services in certain healthcare facilities or through mobile health units. The outcome variable, health care utilization, was defined as the percentage of persons who used health care facilities over the past twelve months.

Table 7.1 presents results of the propensity score matching, Data suggest that the programme has not had a statistically significant impact on utilization of health care services (excluding traditional healers), which paralleled the findings of the World Bank study. Health care utilization appears, in fact, to be lower among project participants than among their matched comparator for all three comparison groups but none of these results are statistically significant.

The self-report exercise attempted to assess the impact on utilization of health care services by asking respondents whether or not they still would have sought medical attention when they were ill if they had not received the health fee exemption or reduction. Table 7.2 presents results of this

Table 7.1 Propensity score matching: impact of health fee exemption/reduction on utilization of healthcare

	Mean difference	Standard error[a]	95% Confidence interval
Nearest match	−0.089	0.060	−0.226–0.020
Nearest three matches	−0.078	0.049	−0.196–0.006
Nearest five matches	−0.077	0.048	−0.176–0.009

[a] Standard errors were bootstrapped with 100 replications.
Data source: Vietnam Household Living Standards Survey (2002).

Table 7.2 Self-reported assessment of use of medical care in Hunger Eradication and Poverty Reduction absence (population proportions, standard errors in parentheses)[a]

	1	2	
	Yes	No	Total
Total Vietnam	91.81 (0.40)	7.28 (0.11)	100

Data do not sum to 100 because 'Don't knows' have been removed.
Data source: HEPR Impact Assessment Qualitative Survey (2003–4).

exercise. The vast majority of respondents maintained that they would have still sought medical care when they were ill even if they had not benefited from the health fee exemption or reduction. Taking into account sampling error, and omitting the 'don't knows' from Table 7.2, up to 95% of respondents said they would have sought medical care. These results are very similar to, and provide an explanation for, those of the propensity score matching. The insignificant impact of this programme on health care utilization rates, relative to non-participants, may simply be because most people would pay for health services in the absence of the programme.

The Tuition and School Maintenance Fee Exemption or Reduction provides students in poor households, as well as certain other eligible groups, exemptions or reductions in the amount they must pay for tuition and the maintenance of schools. The outcome variable, school attendance, was defined as the percentage of children aged 6–17 who attended school over the past twelve months.

Table 7.3 reveals a modest, but statistically significant, impact of the programme on school attendance for all three matched comparisons, which paralleled the findings of the World Bank Study. The impact range is between 3% and 15% depending on the comparison group used and taking into account sampling error.

Table 7.4 presents results of the self-report exercise. Around 12% of respondents claimed that they would not have enrolled their children in primary or secondary school in the absence of the programme. This figure is within the

Table 7.3 Propensity score matching: impact of tuition and school maintenance fee exemption/reduction on school attendance

	Mean difference	Standard error	95% Confidence interval
Nearest match	0.089	0.028	0.032–0.135
Nearest three matches	0.092	0.026	0.060–0.152
Nearest five matches	0.076	0.023	0.037–0.128

Standard errors were bootstrapped with 100 replications.
Data source: Vietnam Household Living Standards Survey (2002).

Table 7.4 Self-reported assessment of primary or secondary enrolment in Hunger Eradication and Poverty Reduction absence (population proportions, standard errors in parentheses)

	1	2	3	
	Yes	No	DK[a]	Total
Total Vietnam	87.64 (1.01)	11.56 (0.32)	0.80 (0.69)	100

[a] Don't know.
Data source: HEPR Impact Assessment Qualitative Survey (2003–4).

range of programme impact found in the propensity score matching exercise which examined *actual* differences in attendance between programme participants and non-participants.

In summary, the HEPR impact assessment combined intersubjectively observable data and thought experiments to determine what would have happened in the absence of the programme. These techniques generated similar results for the education and health project components of HEPR and as such, serve to enhance the overall validity of results. Further, the findings provide preliminary support for the validity of thought experiments as a means of constructing a counterfactual situation though additional research is required to establish their validity across a range of situations.

7.5 Defining Benefits

A final contribution of Q^2 analysis to impact assessment brings us full circle to the issues addressed in Part II of this book on the identification stage of poverty analysis. To recall, discussion focussed on the multiple dimensions of poverty and the rationale for, and implications of, selecting one over another. The analogous issue, in the context of impact assessment, concerns the metric which should be used to gauge programme success or failure. How should project benefits be defined and by whom?

Q^2 analyses have contributed to addressing this question in two ways. First, in the most general sense, a wide range of information sources can inform a broad understanding of the full scope of intended and unintended programme effects and the differentiated impact upon population groups. With respect to the former issue, White (2011) has drawn attention to unintended effects of rural road projects often missed in impact assessments. Drawing on a range of secondary sources, his list of potentially adverse consequences includes increases in traffic accidents, air and noise pollution and opening up an area to military and police control. In terms of affected populations, White argues strongly for disaggregated results based on categories of social differentiation such as caste, gender, ethnicity and so forth, and the nature of livelihood strategies. In Laos, for example, rural roads appear to have increased rural inequality by disproportionately benefitting those able to take advantage of greater market access, including men relative to women.

A second contribution of Q^2 has been to provide a sense of the relative importance of different evaluative metrics for project participants. An example is de Silva and Gunetilleke's (2008) evaluation of resettlement schemes implemented under the Southern Transport Development Project (STDP) in Sri Lanka. This highway development project led to the displacement of around 1,400 households who were subsequently resettled. The methodology included a household survey, with fixed response and open-ended questions, as well as focus group discussions. While the study focussed on monitoring, rather than impact assessment *per se*, it, nevertheless, addressed the relevant issue that 'metrics matter'.

In general terms, household survey data suggested a significant improvement in the quality of new housing provided by the project, as measured by household size, access to toilets, water, and energy. High levels of satisfaction with these amenities were reported. On the other hand, focus group discussions recorded considerable unease with the new living environment due to the loss of a quiet rural environment, coolness, shade, access to fruit, and space for garbage disposal and family burials. Interestingly, the very poor and landless did not share such concerns in that they had limited space previously. According to one respondent: 'in our previous place, we had no place even to spit' (de Silva and Gunetilleke 2008: 258).

A second issue concerned the loss and replacement of land devoted to paddy cultivation. A working assumption among project staff was that such land is not highly valued because paddy cultivation generates very low returns and necessitates arduous effort. The low valuation of paddy land was reflected in the low compensation paid by the project and the fact that households did not replace paddy lands lost to land acquisition in their new surroundings.

A different picture of the local value assigned paddy emerged from the focus group discussions. There was widespread unhappiness about the loss of paddy land. Three factors figured prominently in the discussion. First, there was dissatisfaction with the financial burden of purchasing paddy which had previously been produced on the farm. Second, there was sadness at the ending of an important aspect of social life, sharing the harvest among kin. Finally, there was a pervasive sense of loss at having been dispossessed from land held for generations in one's family. Overall, the assessment of the resettlement experience was much less favourable according to results of focus group discussions than to household survey data. According to the authors (de Silva and Gunetilleke 2008: 260):

> Shared ownership of lands among families, the informal social networks where housework such as child care is often shared, and open access to assets within the extended family, are characteristics of these villages which the STDP has caused to be suddenly severed...A major articulated loss is the loss of the traditional/ ancestral village and the lifestyle that goes with it.

7.6 Conclusion

Impact assessment is about establishing a causal link between programme activities or outputs and development outcomes or impacts. Chapter 5 presented a theoretical case of causal pluralism. It was argued that there are different ways of making causal claims empirically in the social sciences which often rely on different underlying conceptions of causation and models of causal inference. Chapter 6 presented an empirical case which rested on the value-added of Q^2 designs in causal analysis of poverty status and poverty dynamics and in model specification. This chapter has extended the informational base of the empirical case, drawing on Q^2 designs in impact assessment.

More specifically, a number of cases were presented of attempts to combine results and mechanisms which represent the paradigmatic applied case of integrating approaches to causation based on counterfactual dependence and mechanisms. The value added of this design, to explain the reasons underlying observed results, represents one of the key benefits of Q^2 in impact evaluation. Two other categories of approaches were discussed which presented innovative ways of constructing a comparison group or counterfactual scenario, drawing on narrative information, in the case of unmeasured or unobservable variables, and on thought experiments. While these examples leave room for optimism about the role of such approaches, more research is required to establish their validity.

A final category of examples brought us full circle with issues addressed in the identification stage of poverty analysis in Part II of this book, by using Q^2 approaches to investigate if the assessment of programme performance is sensitive to the definition of benefits. The empirical finding, that the 'metric matters' for programme evaluation, are consistent with the findings in Chapter 3 that definitions of poverty matter for the individual households identified as poor.

Overall, the examples reviewed suggest that Q^2 approaches have provided a richer causal analysis of programme benefits by integrating different models of causal inference and by bolstering analyses of counterfactual dependence. As such, they have contributed to enriching our understanding of the core questions of impact assessment, namely 'who benefits, how much, and why?' Once again, such studies support the empirical case for causal pluralism.

Part IV
Conclusion

Chapter 8

Conclusion

The large body of mixed-method, or Q^2, research on poverty conducted over the past decade has served as an entry point for a two-pronged line of inquiry undertaken in this book. First, it allowed for an investigation of foundational assumptions, concerning epistemology and causation, which underlie approaches to poverty. Second, it facilitated a critical review of the wide range of tools and methods within the social sciences which may be used to understand and explain social phenomena, such as poverty, and the ways they may be fruitfully combined. Both such inquiries contributed to the core objective of examining the underlying assumptions and implications of how we conceptualize and investigate poverty.

Of the many issues raised throughout this book, two central messages stand out. First, foundations matter. Foundational assumptions have implications for the conceptual categories and analytical lens we use. They determine what counts as reliable knowledge and 'hard' evidence, how to ascertain validity, how causation is defined and causal claims established empirically and so forth. Foundations also matter for research results, when, for example, different approaches to poverty come to different conclusions about 'who is poor' or different conceptions of causation arrive at different conclusions about the causal impact of development programmes. Section 8.1 reviews the evidence in support of the conclusion that foundations matter.

The second central message is that mixed method analyses add value. Throughout this book, many examples were provided where Q^2 approaches strengthened poverty analysis. In the identification stage, such approaches facilitated incorporating locally meaningful definitions, weights, and thresholds of poverty in ways that addressed requirements of interpersonal comparability, specifically 'basket' and 'levels' consistency, and external validity. In the causal stage, Q^2 studies have added value by improving, and/or broadening, analysis of four aspects of the causal framework, namely causal variables, weights, mechanisms, and the causal 'tree', while also addressing issues of external validity. A selective review of some of the best examples of value added is presented in Section 8.2.

Section 8.3 concludes with a case for methodological pluralism drawing primarily on the evidence presented throughout this book.

8.1 Foundations Matter

It has been argued throughout this book that foundations matter in two ways. First, they determine the conceptual categories and analytical approaches used to understand and explain social phenomena. Second, they have implications for research results if different approaches to poverty or to causation, for example, generate conflicting findings.

8.1.1 Conceptual Categories and Analytical Approaches

The first point was illustrated in Parts II and III of this book in the discussion of the identification and causal stages of poverty analysis respectively. In terms of identification, which addresses the questions 'Who are the poor?' and 'What are their characteristics?', it was argued that epistemological considerations, related to Empiricism and hermeneutics, or critical hermeneutics, explain aspects of the consumption and dialogical approaches to poverty.

For the consumption approach, the commitment to Empiricism helps explain the core unit of knowledge, a brute datum, and the validity criteria, intersubjective observability, used in utility theory and nutrition science. Specifically, utilitarianism and utility theory made the object of value, happiness and subsequently preference fulfilment, a brute datum known without recourse to non-empirical entities. Further, levels of preference fulfilment became intersubjectively observable, through revealed preference theory, and allegedly amenable to interpersonal comparison, through money metric utility. Nutrition science allowed for the estimation of adequacy levels of caloric intake though controlled experiments based on brute data. The result is the conception of consumption poverty, anchored on inadequate caloric intake and measured by low levels of consumption expenditure. In this tradition of inquiry, determining the validity of statements about consumption poverty hinges on the intersubjectively observable nature of poverty data.

There are no such intermediate bodies of theory underlying the dialogical approach to poverty. Nevertheless, there are important similarities between its conceptualization of poverty and that of hermeneutics and critical hermeneutics. Intersubjective meanings substitute for brute data as the core unit of knowledge, while a discourse-based model of validity based on the characteristics of actual dialogue substitutes for an observation-based model. As a consequence, the dialogical approach places emphasis on understanding diverse and local meanings of poverty and in creating conditions to facilitate more genuine, participatory dialogue. Differences of this sort are important because they have decided implications for the way we address the questions 'Who are the poor?' and 'What are their characteristics?'.

Foundations also matter in the causal stage of poverty analysis, because they have bearing on the chosen conception or causation and model of causal inference. A core distinction was drawn in Chapter 5 between approaches to causation which are 'difference-makers' and those which are 'producers.' In the first case, causation is 'making more likely', or increasingly the probability of an event or a probabilistic association between variables. In the second case, causation involves a process of generation and is closely related to the ideas of transitivity and locality. Transitivity holds that if 'a' causes 'b', and 'b' causes 'c', then 'a' is a cause of 'c' while locality maintains that causes and effects are linked by a continuous series of intermediate events linked in time and space.

Three approaches to causation were examined namely, conditional association and counterfactual dependence, which are 'difference-makers', and mechanism-based approaches which are 'producers'. The first two approaches constitute the foundations of econometric models of poverty and experimental or quasi-experimental approaches to impact assessment, respectively. The latter is the underpinning of those empirical approaches which rely on dialogical inquiry to make causal claims. The key point is that the three approaches represent different ways of understanding what it means for 'a' to cause 'b', and different ways of inferring such causal relations empirically. Such differences are important because they bear on how we understand, and go about answering, the question 'why are people poor'

8.1.2 *Research Results*

Foundations also matter for research results. In the identification stage, the core question is whether consumption and dialogical approaches to poverty identify different population groups, with different characteristics, as poor because of their epistemological underpinnings. The first-generation of Q^2 work reviewed in Chapter 3, addressed this question empirically though combined analysis of poverty using consumption and dialogical approaches. The core conclusion of these studies was that foundational differences between consumption and dialogical approaches do indeed account, in part, for the different empirical results which they generate.

Specifically, wide divergences were found with respect to the individual households identified as poor and certain of their characteristics, along with estimates of overall poverty levels and trends. It was noted that there are many potential reasons for these divergent results relating to population coverage, intrahousehold issues, visibility bias, recall/nostalgia biases, and so on. The one empirical study which has attempted to ascertain the relative importance of different explanations such as these found that foundational differences concerning underlying definitions of poverty accounted for over half of the contrasting findings

Foundations may also matter for research results in causal analysis. The point was illustrated in Section 5.1, by contrasting experimental and non-experimental approaches to impact assessment in terms of a hypothetical micro-credit project as well as debates about substitution bias. To recall, consider two micro-credit projects, '*a*' and '*b*', which together supply credit to all members of a population. Access to credit from project '*a*' precludes, that is 'pre-empts,' access to project '*b*' and vice versa. Assume that both projects, and not other factors, succeed in significantly raising income, '*c*', of project participants in identical fashion. In this example, project '*a*' causes '*c*' in terms of 'production', in that it increased the income of project participants, but not in terms of 'difference-making', in that project '*b*' produced identical results.

Debates about substitution bias are another way of illustrating this issue. In the context of experimental approaches to impact assessment, substitution bias occurs when non-programme participants, who are members of the control group for the evaluation of project 'a', can participate in another, substitute programme 'b'. According to James Heckman (2000: 83) the effect is a 'gross underestimation of the program's effectiveness'. Thomas Cook (2000: 79), on the other hand, argues that 'it makes little sense to criticize [random assignment] for substitution bias... After all, experiments answer the question of whether a treatment is better than some alternative'. While this exchange is phrased in terms of the correct counterfactual to use, it can alternatively be interpreted as a debate as to whether or not the impact of a programme should be assessed in terms of difference-making or in terms of some notion of production.

Foundations do matter for the conceptual categories and analytical approaches we use and for research results. This conclusion has important implications for the case for methodological pluralism presented in Section 8.3.

8.2 Mixed Methods Add Value

The second core message of this book is that mixed methods add value for understanding and explaining social phenomena. Many examples were provided in Chapter 4, which addressed identification issues, and Chapters 6 and 7, which focused on causation. In this section, a few examples of such value-added from both the identification and causal stages of poverty analysis will be reviewed. The organizing framework draws on Jennifer Greene and colleague's (1989) typology of mixed-method approaches discussed in Section 1.3.

To recall, Greene distinguished a number of purposes of mixed method research, four of which are relevant, namely development, triangulation, complementarity, and expansion. Development refers to the use of methods from one approach to assist in the methodological development of another through say, using focus groups to better structure the wording of fixed response surveys. Triangulation uses different of methods to investigate the same phenomenon to assess, and/or bolster, the validity of research results. Complementarity relies on different methodological approaches to clarify, elaborate upon or better interpret the results of one method with those of another. Finally, expansion refers to the use of different methods to address related, but distinct, components of an overall research question such as the combined analysis of outcomes and processes.

8.2.1 Development

All of the studies in Chapter 4 are examples of development whereby locally meaningful poverty definitions, thresholds, and weights derived from dialogical inquiry were integrated in studies which attempted to satisfy the requirements of interpersonal comparability and external validity. A number of different approaches were presented. In Barahona and Levy's (2007) study in Malawi, locally meaningful definitions of poverty related to food insecurity, drawn from Participatory Rural Appraisals (PRAs), were included into a probabilistically sampled household survey. In Howe and McKay's (2007) analysis in Rwanda, characteristics of chronic poverty uncovered in a Participatory Poverty Assessment (PPA) with national scope were 'mapped' onto similar indicators included in a nationally representative household survey. In another approach, by Hargreaves et al. (2007) in South Africa, data on the characteristics of the poor from wealth rankings exercises were transformed numerically on the basis of the frequency with which they were mentioned, allowing for the calculation of a household wealth index. Many other examples were presented with reference to weights and thresholds.

Development also figured centrally in forms of causal analysis, in particular econometric modelling. Section 6.5 presented examples of the use of narrative information from semi-structured interviews to facilitate model specification. In one example, by Rao et al. (2003) in India, narrative information served to identify an instrumental value which could be used to estimate the effects of condom use on the revenue of sex workers. Another example by Quisumbing (2011) from Bangladesh showed how dialogical information concerning the combined importance of dowry and illness led to the respecification of an econometric model by including an interaction term comprising these two variables.

The developmental function of mixed method analysis illustrates the pragmatic case for methodological pluralism presented in Section 8.3. There is good reason to draw on a wide range of informational sources if they can assist in the methodological development of a particular approach.

8.2.2 Triangulation

Triangulation is about investigating the same phenomena using different methodological approaches to determine if they arrive at similar research results. Most of the first generation Q^2 studies fall under this heading in that they sought to determine if identification of the poor and their characteristics, along with estimates of poverty levels and trends, depends on the approach adopted. Such inquiry does not strictly meet the definition of triangulation because the phenomena under examination are not the same, namely consumption poverty on the one hand and a multidimensional, discursively generated definition of poverty on the other. Nevertheless, they are related and fall broadly under the category of deprivation. As discussed in Chapter 4 and Section 8.1, a common finding from this literature is that the way poverty is defined matters for identification of the poor and their characteristics, and for estimates of poverty levels and trends. Accordingly, consumption poverty does not serve as a good proxy for deprivation *tout court*.

In terms of causation, a good example of triangulation was found in the impact assessment of the Hunger Eradication and Poverty Reduction (HEPR) programme in Vietnam, discussed in Section 7.4 (Shaffer 2012). The study combined propensity score-matching techniques using intersubjectively observable data with thought experiments to determine what would have happened in the absence of the programme. Thought experiments took the form of subjunctive conditional (if–then) questions posed about what respondents would have done in the absence of the programme. The two approaches generated quite similar results for the education and health project components of HEPR and, as such, served to enhance the overall validity of results. Further, the findings provided preliminary support for the validity of thought experiments as a means of constructing a counterfactual situation.

The triangulation function of Q^2 research is quite integral to the case for methodological pluralism given real-world problems of empirical adjudication discussed in Section 8.3.

8.2.3 *Complementarity*

Complementarity was found in causal analysis of poverty, whereby the results of dialogical inquiry and participant observation were used to better interpret the results of statistical analyses of household survey data. Examples were found in both causal analysis of poverty status and poverty dynamics, model specification, and impact assessment.

One example was Woldehanna *et al.*'s (2005) study of child labour in Ethiopia discussed in Section 6.3.1, which combined econometric analysis of household survey data with findings from semi-structured interviews. The latter provided explanations for a number of counterintuitive findings such as the association between higher maternal education and the likelihood of child labour. Semi-structured interview results suggested that this finding may have been because women with higher levels of education are more likely to work outside their homes, which increases the domestic work burden of older children who assume responsibility for childcare and other tasks.

A second example is de Weerdt's (2010) study of poverty dynamics in Tanzania, presented in Section 6.5.2, which combined econometric analysis of panel data with narrative information from focus group discussions and life histories. The econometric analysis predicted 2004 asset values of households on the basis of household characteristics in 1990, while the narrative information explained why certain households had 'defied their economic destiny'. Specifically, the dialogic information pointed to intervening events between waves of the panel such as agricultural shocks, mortality, illness, and widowhood or death along with variables not included in the survey such as alcoholism, bad marital relations, and lack of exposure to outside information. Further, life histories and focus groups suggested that the interaction between initial conditions and remoteness was particularly important because unfavourable initial conditions could be overcome in non-remote villages. Such information led to the specification of the causal structure of the econometric model by including an interaction term between remoteness and initial conditions which proved to be statistically significant.

A last example involved the use of statistical analysis of household survey data to better contextualize the results of ethnographic inquiry. The study by Place *et al.* (2007) discussed in Section 6.3.1 examined the adoption and effects of new agro-forestry technologies on the poor in rural Kenya. The household survey data facilitated the distinction between outlier and tendency cases with respect to both adoption and benefits of the new agricultural technology. For example, household survey data allowed for the statistical analysis of associations between poverty measures and the uptake of new technologies which could not have been undertaken using data from the ethnographies because of the small number of observations.

As with triangulation, complementarity is central to the case for methodological pluralism in light of its role in empirical adjudication between research results, and in facilitating understanding of complex phenomena, discussed in Section 8.3.

8.2.4 *Expansion*

In the broader literature on mixed methods, expansion represents one of the paradigmatic ways that mixed method approaches have been fruitfully combined. In terms of Q^2, it was found primarily in causal analysis, specifically in the joint investigation of causal outcomes and processes. The outcome/process distinction in causal analysis of poverty status or dynamics, discussed in chapter 6, is analogous to the distinction between results and mechanisms in impact assessment, examined in Section 7.2. Both derived from the distinction between two concepts of causation, namely 'difference-makers' and 'producers', outlined in Section 5.1.

A number of good examples were found in the literature. Baulch and Davis' (2008) study in Bangladesh combined panel data with life histories. The panel data allowed for econometric analysis on determinants of poverty transitions and consumption expenditure per capita. The life histories provided a much richer depiction of the nature of trajectories of change and the forces generating them. Four patterns of change emerged from the narrative information, described as 'smooth, saw-tooth, single step and multi-step processes', which are either upward or downward trending. The Q^2 design integrated causal weights from the econometric analysis with a rich depiction of causal mechanisms and the causal tree from the life histories. Accordingly, it represents the combined use of approaches to causation based on conditional association and mechanisms.

A second example is provided by the International Food Policy Research Institute's impact assessment of the Social Risk Mitigation Programme in Turkey (Adato 2008). Household survey data on educational outcomes revealed low rates of secondary enrolment for girls. Ethnographic work, involving semi-structured interviews and participant observation, provided information on some of the underlying reasons. For girls, the potential employment or wage effect of additional schooling was not highly valued given the overriding importance of their traditional female roles as mothers and wives. Further, concerns were raised about threats to family honour and reputation associated with girls' schooling. The core contribution of the ethnographic work was to provide an account of the mechanisms generating results about programme impact.

Expansion is quite important to the case for methodological pluralism discussed in Section 8.3, in that it directs attention to the imperative of using a range of methodological approaches to facilitate understanding of complex social phenomena.

Overall, the conclusions of this book about the value added of Q^2 echo very strongly the findings of the 2004 Q^2 conference at the University of Toronto. The conference organizers argued that:

> This recent rediscovery of mixed methods in poverty analysis is a welcome development with large potential payoffs in terms of understanding and explaining poverty. There are many examples of value-added associated with mixing found in the contributions to this Symposium, such as the use of 'qualitative' information to: improve household survey design; interpret counterintuitive or surprising findings from household surveys; explain the reasons behind observed outcomes; probe motivations underlying observed behavior; suggest the direction of causality; assess the validity of quantitative results; better understand conceptual categories such as labor, the household etc.; facilitate analysis of locally meaningful categories of social differentiation; provide a dynamic dimension to one-off household survey data, etc.... In our view, the benefits of mixing are not in doubt. (Kanbur and Shaffer 2007: 183–184)

8.3 A Case for Methodological Pluralism

This book has examined the underlying assumptions and implications of how we conceptualize and investigate poverty. It has addressed foundational and applied issues. Foundational differences related to epistemology and causation were identified and linked to applied approaches in the identification and causal stages of poverty analysis. It was argued that foundations matter for the conceptual categories and analytical approaches we use, and for research results. It was also argued that empirical literature is replete with examples of value-added for understanding and explaining poverty through the use of Q^2 research designs.

Together, the various lines of inquiry presented in this book make a case for methodological pluralism. This case does not attempt to integrate broader arguments for methodological pluralism found in other literatures such as philosophy (Roth 1987) or economics (Dow 2004). It is simply a way of summing up key themes presented in this book, and takes the form of four interrelated arguments.

First, it has been argued that foundational assumptions determine our conceptual categories and analytical lens. One implication is that our foundational priors determine, in part, how we understand the world and what we see. They drive the questions posed, and not posed, and the ways of answering them. In terms of poverty analysis, our priors determine how we define poverty, as discussed in Part II, and how we understand and empirically investigate its causes, as examined in Part III. In fact, part of the theoretical case for causal pluralism presented in Section 5.1 rested on just such different intuitions about the meaning of causation, encapsulated in the distinction between 'difference-makers' and 'producers'. As discussed in Section 8.1, our chosen conceptual and analytical lenses also have implications for research results.

The key point is that all knowledge is partial. The first argument in favour of methodological pluralism, then, is simply that there are strong reasons not to unduly restrict the field of inquiry to any one partial analytical perspective. Otherwise, we arbitrarily create blinders, and miss out on potentially relevant information. The resulting bias has been labelled, in cognitive psychology, the so-called WYSIATI principle—'what you see is all there is' (Kahneman 2012: 85–88). In terms of research findings and policy recommendations, an analogous WYSIWYG principle applies: 'what you see is what you get'.

Not only is knowledge partial, it is also fallible and adjudication between conflicting results is often inconclusive. The second argument in favour of methodological pluralism rests on the role of mixed methods in facilitating the process of empirical validation of research findings or adjudication between conflicting results. Little (1998: 173) aptly paraphrases some of the difficulties involved in establishing the validity of our knowledge claims:

> Scientific disputes are inherently underdetermined by the evidence. There are no pure 'facts,' but only facts as couched in one conceptual scheme or another. There are no pure observations, but rather observations couched in a theory-laden vocabulary. Theories bring with them their own empirical criteria, which bias the findings in support of them. The relations between observation and theory are hopelessly circular, with theories generating the observations that supposedly support them.

Similar types of difficulties in empirical adjudication of knowledge claims were found in the identification and causal stages of poverty analysis. With respect to the identification stage, it was argued, in Sections 2.5 and 2.6, that different validity criteria apply when assessing findings of the consumption and dialogical approaches to poverty. In terms of the causal stage, different conceptions of causation and attendant models of causal inference have been used to infer the causes of poverty or the causal effect of development projects. As discussed in Section 8.1, such differences can account for different research findings.

It is in this context, that mixed methods have a potentially important role to play in the process of empirical adjudication. As discussed in Section 8.2 under the heading 'triangulation', the case for the validity of research results is strengthened if different methodological approaches applied to the same research question arrive at similar conclusions. An example was the use of two different ways of constructing a counterfactual scenario in the impact assessment of Vietnam's HEPR programme, based on intersubjectively observable data and thought experiments. As it happens, the two approaches generated quite similar results for the education and health project components of HEPR and, as such, served to enhance the overall validity of results.

A third argument shifts from the nature of knowledge to characteristics of the social world. The process of understanding and explaining is greatly complicated by the complexity of the phenomena under examination. The point was first illustrated in Part II in the examination of the wide range of local meanings associated with the word poverty, along with the interrelationship between their various dimensions.

The inherent complexity of social phenomena was brought our more forcefully in the discussion of causation. Causation is exceedingly complex. There is an almost infinite range of potential causal variables which are interacting with one another in ways which are hard to understand. There are good reasons to believe that the combined use of a number of approaches to causation is necessary to provide an adequate account of the multiple features of the causal framework, which include causal variables, weights, mechanisms, and the causal tree. As argued by Nancy Cartwright and others, as discussed in Section 5.1, there is no singular concept of causation, or model of causal inference, that does justice to the wide varieties of causal phenomena in the world. Further, combining approaches to causal inquiry can serve to illuminate different aspects of the underlying causal structure and relationships and, in principle, enrich causal analysis. If fact, the review of the Q^2 literature was replete with examples where mixing methods served to improve or broaden causal analysis. Some such examples were discussed under the headings of 'complementarity' and 'expansion' in Section 8.2.

The final argument for methodological pluralism is the pragmatic case. Mixed methods work. They can lead to better understanding and explanation. They are many such examples in the literature which appear throughout this book. Section 8.2 provided a select review of the range of value-added which mixed methods can provide.

This favourable assessment does not mean that mixed methods always work. The examples presented throughout this book have been deliberately selected because of their high quality. Further, it does not mean that mixed methods are always necessary for understanding or explanation. The choice of method should depend on the research question at hand. Still, examples of value-added abound in the literature. Accordingly, it would be odd to arbitrarily restrict the methodological choice set to a single approach at the onset.

The summary case for methodological pluralism, then, rests on four claims. Knowledge is partial. Empirical adjudication is imperfect. The world is complex. Mixed methods add value. They are many ways to understand the world, all of which have strengths and limitations. Ultimately, the goals of understanding and explanation are best served if research questions dictate choice of methodological approach rather than the other way around.

Appendix 1

Q² Research Designs and Methods

The purpose of this appendix is to provide a quick reference guide to the main approaches to poverty analysis reviewed in Chapters 4, 6, and 7 of this book. The order of the studies follows the format of these chapters, beginning with the identification stage of poverty analysis before proceeding to the causal stage. Summary information on the methods, data sources, and value-added are presented.

We also include in the summary table information on the purpose of the Q² design using Jennifer Greene and colleague's (1989) typology discussed in Sections 1.3 and 8.2. Four of their five listed purposes of mixed-method research are relevant, namely development, triangulation, complementarity, and expansion. To recall, development refers to the use of methods from one approach to assist in the methodological development of another through, say, using focus groups to better structure the wording of fixed response surveys. Triangulation uses different methods to investigate the same phenomenon to assess, and/or bolster, the validity of research results. Complementarity relies on different methodological approaches to clarify, elaborate upon or better interpret the results of one method with those of another. Finally, expansion refers to the use of different methods to address related, but distinct, components of an overall research question such as the combined analysis of outcomes and processes.

A.1 Identification: Who are the Poor and What are their Characteristics?

A.1.1 *Operationalizing Dimensions of Poverty*
The studies in this section attempt to integrate locally meaningful definitions of poverty in a way which facilitates interpersonal comparisons and, in many cases, external validity of results. A common design is to combine information from dialogical inquiry with household survey data or to transform data numerically, or statistically, to facilitate interpersonal comparability.

Appendix

Authors	Data sources	Purpose (Greene *et al.* 1989)	Description and Q² value-added
Barahona and Levy (2007)	PRAs Household surveys	Development	Locally meaningful definitions of poverty related to food insecurity, drawn from Participatory Rural Appraisals (PRAs), were included into a probabilistically sampled household survey. The value added of Q^2 was to (i) include locally meaningful definitions of deprivation; (ii) enhance comparability of results over different populations by using the same definition of poverty; (iii) achieve external validity of results through probabilistic sampling.
Sharp and Devereux (2004)	Group discussion Household surveys	Development	Group discussions among teams of 'qualitative' and 'quantitative' researchers operationalized the concept of destitution, which was subsequently included into a probabilistically sampled household survey. The value added of Q^2 was to (i) include locally meaningful definitions of destitution; (ii) enhance comparability of results over different populations by using the same definition of destitution; (iii) achieve external validity of results through probabilistic sampling.
Howe and McKay (2007)	PPAs household surveys	Development	Characteristics of chronic poverty uncovered in a Participatory Poverty Assessment (PPA) with national scope were 'mapped' onto similar indicators included in a nationally representative household survey. The value added of Q^2 was to (i) rely on locally meaningful characteristics of chronic poverty; (ii) enhance comparability of results over different populations by using common correlates of chronic poverty; (iii) achieve external validity of results through probabilistic sampling.
Hargreaves *et al.* (2007)	PPAs	Development	Data on the characteristics of the poor from wealth rankings exercises were transformed numerically on the basis of the frequency with which they were mentioned, allowing for the calculation of a household wealth index. The value added of Q^2 was to (i) rely on locally meaningful information on characteristics of poverty; (ii) enhance comparability of results over different populations by numerically transforming this information.
Campenhout (2006)	PPAs	Development	Well-being ranking results from PPAs were adjusted statistically by controlling for village and sub-village effects which could bias interpersonal comparisons. The value added of Q^2 was to (i) rely on locally meaningful definitions of poverty reflected in well-being rankings; (ii) enhance comparability of results over different populations by statistically adjusting this information.

(continued)

(Continued)

Authors	Data sources	Purpose (Greene et al. 1989)	Description and Q^2 value-added
Beegle et al. (2009)	Household surveys	Development	Household survey respondents were asked to situated themselves on a six-step well-being ladder and respond to a series of 'vignettes' in which they placed four hypothetical families on the same ladder. Data from the vignettes were then used, inter alia, to rescale responses to the first question to facilitate interpersonal comparability. The value added of Q^2 was to (i) rely on people's perceptions about the level of their own well-being; (ii) enhance comparability of results over different populations by statistically adjusting this information; (iii) achieve external validity of results through probabilistic sampling.

A.1.2 Weighting Dimensions of Poverty

The studies in this section aim to rely on locally meaningful weighting scheme to determine the relative importance of various dimensions of poverty. A core distinction is between indirect approaches, which rely on econometric analysis of correlates of well-being rankings, and direct approaches in which respondents are asked to provide the weights directly.

Authors	Data sources	Purpose (Greene et al. 1989)	Description and Q^2 value-added
Kebede (2009)	PPAs Household Surveys	Development	Well-being ranking results from PPAs and observable household characteristics from household surveys were combined with econometric analysis of the correlates of different ranking groups. The authors interpret the regression coefficients as an indication of the social value, or weight, afforded characteristics such as income, assets, land, number of adults and housing. The value added of Q^2 was to used statistical analysis of household survey data to infer, weights used in well-being rankings.
de Kruijk and Rutten (2007)	Household surveys	Development	A nationally representative household survey was administered which asked respondents to rank twelve dimensions of well-being in terms of their perceived priority. Rankings were averaged separately for men and women and relative weights calculated for use in the Human Vulnerability Index. The value added of Q^2 was to (i) rely on people's perceptions about the relative importance of dimensions of well-being; (ii) achieve external validity of results through probabilistic sampling.

(continued)

(Continued)

Authors	Data sources	Purpose (Greene *et al.* 1989)	Description and Q^2 value-added
Woodcock *et al.* (2009)	Household survey	Development	The development of the Wellbeing Research in Developing Countries Quality of Life Questionnaire (WEDQoL) in Thailand began with an exploratory phase where respondents were posed open-ended questions about the sources of happiness. Results were subsequently codified into 51 items in the fixed response WEDQoL, and respondents asked to rate them in terms of their perceived necessity for well-being. The core value added of Q^2 was to rely on people's ratings of the relative importance of dimensions of well-being to elicit weights.
Esposito *et al.* (2012)	Focus group discussions Household surveys	Development	Focus group discussions were held to elicit a short-list of highly valued literary practices. Such practices were then included in a household survey which respondents were asked to simultaneously rank by allocating fifty beans amongst them. Unlike sequential ranking in the two aforementioned studies, simultaneous ranking forces respondents to jointly valuate the importance of all five practices. The core value added of Q^2 was to rely on people's simultaneous ratings of the relative importance of literary practices.

A.1.3 *Setting Poverty Thresholds*

Q^2 analyses have attempted to set the poverty line at a point which reflects locally meaningful thresholds. The studies in this section present three different approaches based on data discontinuities, conceptual thresholds and the 'consumption adequacy' question.

Authors	Data sources	Purpose (Greene *et al.* 1989)	Description and Q^2 value-added
Hargreaves *et al.* (2007)	PPA	Development	Drawing on PPA data, analysis was conducted to determine if particular statements were overwhelmingly made about the poor, very poor and other well-being groups. Such 'data discontinuities' were detected by visual inspection and used to distinguish thresholds between well-being groups. The core value-added of Q^2 was to base poverty thresholds on local perceptions of the characteristics of poverty.
Barahona and Levy (2007)	PPA Household survey	Development	There is a built-in 'conceptual threshold' associated with the idea of 'not having enough food' used as the poverty measure in the household survey, drawing on results of a prior PPA. The core value added of Q^2 was to base food security thresholds on local perceptions of adequacy.

(continued)

(Continued)

Authors	Data sources	Purpose (Greene *et al.* 1989)	Description and Q² value-added
Pradhan and Ravallion (2000)	Household survey	Development	A consumption adequacy question (CAQ) was posed in households surveys, whereby respondents we asked if their level of consumption (food, housing, clothing, etc.) is more than, less than, or just adequate to meet family needs. By regressing responses to the CAQ on consumption expenditure, subjective consumption poverty lines were calculated. The core value added of Q² was to base the consumption poverty line on people's perceptions of consumption adequacy.

A.2 Causal Analysis of Poverty Status and Dynamics

A.2.1 *Determinants of Poverty Status—I: Combining Outcomes and Processes*

The studies in this section illustrate one of the major contributions of Q² research to causal analysis, namely to combine analyses of outcomes and processes. Such analyses have improved, or broadened, aspects of the causal framework, including causal variables, weights, mechanisms and the causal 'tree', while also directing attention to issues of external validity, as discussed in Section 6.1.

Authors	Data Sources	Purpose (Greene *et al.* 1989)	Description and Q² value-added
Place *et al.* (2007)	Ethnographies Household surveys	Complementarity Expansion	Examination of the effect of agricultural technologies on the poor which combined an analysis of outcomes, drawing on panel data from household surveys, with processes relying on semi-structured interviews and participant observation. The value added of Q² was to (i) distinguish between outlier and tendency cases; (ii) help interpret the meaning of variables in the household survey; (iii) probe the reasons for the testing and adoption of new technology; (iv) explain counter-intuitive results from the household survey. The Q² design enhanced or facilitated the understanding of causal variables, mechanisms and the causal tree and allowed for an assessment of the external validity of the ethnographic results

(continued)

(Continued)

Authors	Data Sources	Purpose (Greene *et al.* 1989)	Description and Q^2 value-added
Woldehanna *et al.* (2005)	Household surveys Semi-structured interviews	Complementarity Expansion	Econometric analysis of household survey data on correlates of child schooling and labour was followed-up by semi-structured interviews to provide a richer understanding of the statistical results. The core value added of Q^2 was to explain the reasons for counterintuitive econometric results and, in the process, provide a fuller account of causal mechanisms and the causal tree.

A.2.2 *Determinants of poverty status—II: the rural livelihoods approach*

The series of studies in this section rely on the sustainable livelihoods framework whereby 'forms of capital' or assets are transformed into livelihoods via mediating processes related to social relations, institutions, and so on. Q^2 research has been used to highlight different elements of this overall analytical framework.

Authors	Data sources	Purpose (Greene *et al.* 1989)	Description and Q^2 Value-added
Ellis and Freeman (2004)	PRAs Household surveys	Complementarity Expansion	Household survey data on assets, incomes, shocks and livelihood activities were combined with information from the PRAs on mediating processes, related primarily to institutions, to enrich the overall analysis. The core value added of Q^2 was to explain the reasons for some of the descriptive statistical findings from the household surveys and, in the process, provide a fuller account of causal mechanisms and the causal tree.

A.2.3 *Determinants of poverty dynamics—I: interviewing the transition matrix*

Poverty dynamics, or the flows of households into and out of poverty, can be represented in terms of a poverty transition matrix, which distinguishes between households who remain poor, escape from poverty, enter into poverty, and remain non-poor. All of the Q^2 studies in this section have contributed to a fuller explanation, and better understanding, of this transition matrix.

Authors	Data sources	Purpose (Greene et al. 1989)	Description and Q^2 value-added
Barrett et al. (2006)	Household Surveys Oral histories Semi-structured interviews	Complementarity Expansion	Econometric analysis was conducted to test for the existence of poverty traps and detailed case studies subsequently undertaken of households within the transition matrix to uncover the reasons behind well-being trajectories. The core value added of Q^2 was to integrate causal weights and mechanisms with a more detailed account of the causal tree.
Baulch and Davis (2008)	Household surveys Life histories	Complementarity Expansion	Descriptive statistical and econometric analysis of panel data were combined with life histories of households in different quadrants of the transition matrix to provide a richer depiction of trajectories of change. The core value added of Q^2 was to integrate causal weights and mechanisms with a more detailed account of the causal tree.
Adato et al. (2006, 2007)	Household surveys Oral histories Semi-structured interviews	Complementarity Expansion	Similar to Barrett et al. (2006), econometric analysis was conducted to test for the existence of poverty traps and detailed case studies subsequently undertaken of households to uncover the reasons behind well-being trajectories. The core value added of Q^2 was to integrate causal weights and mechanisms with a more detailed account of causal variables and the causal tree.

A.2.4 Determinants of poverty dynamics—II: the 'Stages of Progress' approach

Causal analysis using the Stages of Progress (SoP) methodology entails, first, situating households within the poverty transition matrix using recall, second, eliciting reasons for escape from, and descents into, poverty, and, third, modelling 'reasons' econometrically (Krishna 2010b). The Q^2 contribution in the studies in this section has been to identify causal variables and to assign causal weights.

Authors	Data Sources	Purpose (Greene et al. 1989)	Description and Q^2 value-added
Krishna et al. (2006a) Krishna et al. (2006b)	Focus group discussions Semi-structured interviews	Development Expansion Triangulation	Following identification of the main reasons for well-being trajectories, logistic (logit) regression models were estimated of the likelihood of falling into, or escaping, poverty using the previously uncovered variables. The core value added of Q^2 was to integrate causal weights and mechanisms with a more detailed account of causal variables.

(continued)

125

(Continued)

Authors	Data Sources	Purpose (Greene et al. 1989)	Description and Q^2 value-added
Krishna and Lecy (2008)	Focus group discussions Semi-structured interviews	Development Expansion Triangulation	A 'net events' variable, which is the difference between positive and negative events or 'reasons', was calculated and included in econometric analysis of the determinants of well-being transitions. The core value added of Q^2 was to integrate causal weights and mechanisms with a more detailed account of causal variables and the causal tree.

A2.5 Model specification

The studies in this section provide examples of how various types of narrative information have proved useful for purposes of econometric modelling, by facilitating selection of causal variables and specification of the causal tree.

Authors	Data Sources	Purpose (Greene et al. 1989)	Description and Q^2 value-added
Rao et al. (2003)	Focus group discussions Household surveys	Development	Results of focus group discussions facilitated the selection of an 'instrumental variable' for inclusion in an econometric model of the effects of condom use on revenue among sex workers. The core value added of Q^2 was to aid in the specification of causal variables.
de Weerdt (2010)	Focus group discussions Life histories Household surveys	Development Complementarity Expansion	Econometric analysis, conducted to predict 2004 asset values on the basis of 1993 household characteristics, was combined with dialogical methods to explain why certain households had 'defied their economic destiny'. The dialogical methods facilitated identification of an interaction variable between remoteness and initial conditions which was subsequently used in econometric modelling. The value added of Q^2 was to aid in the specification of causal variables and their interrelationships, or the causal tree, along with an understanding of the underlying causal mechanisms at work.

(continued)

(Continued)

Authors	Data Sources	Purpose (Greene et al. 1989)	Description and Q^2 value-added
Quisumbing (2011)	Focus group discussions Household surveys	Development Expansion	Focus group discussions facilitated the specification of variables which were subsequently included in a household survey, along with the construction of interaction terms which were included in the econometric modelling. The core value added of Q^2 was to aid in the specification of causal variables and understanding of the causal tree.

A.3 Causal analysis in impact assessment

A.3.1 Combining results and mechanisms

The studies in this section illustrate how Q^2 research designs have allowed for the combined examination of the magnitude of impact, or 'results', and the underlying reasons, or 'mechanisms'.

Authors	Data sources	Purpose (Greene et al. 1989)	Description and Q^2 value-added
Adato (2008)	Semi-structured interviews Participant observation Household Surveys	Complementarity Expansion	Experimental and quasi-experimental (regression discontinuity techniques) analyses of household survey data were combined with the results of ethnographic research to present a combined study of the magnitude of, and reasons for, impact.
Broegaard et al. (2011)	Focus group discussions Semi-structured interviews Household surveys	Complementarity Expansion	Quasi-experimental analysis (propensity score matching) of household survey data was combined with narrative information from semi-structured interviews and focus group discussions to present a combined study of the magnitude of, and reasons for, impact.

A.3.2 *Identifying comparison groups*

The studies in this section illustrate how Q^2 approaches, specifically various forms of narrative information, are used to assist in the formation of comparison groups.

Authors	Data Sources	Purpose (Greene et al. 1989)	Description and Q^2 value-added
Ravallion (2001)	Narrative information Household surveys	Development	A chance encounter between Ms Analyst and Ms Sensible Sociologist reveals information on the determinants of programme participation, specifically budgetary allocation to school boards. A budget allocation variable could be subsequently used to estimate a model of programme participation and as an 'instrument' in a model of schooling.
Rao and Ibáñez's (2005)	Focus group discussions Semi-structured interviews Household survey	Development	In the first stage matching, narrative information was used to select five similar communities to those included in the study incorporating 'unmeasured' variables such the number of churches and youth groups, and 'unobservables' such as political culture and social structure. The authors maintain that use of these additional sources of information contributed to minimising the problem of selection bias.

A.3.3 *Conducting counterfactual thought experiments*

In this study, a counterfactual scenario was constructed by way of a though experiment relying on perceptual data from household surveys and compared with results of a propensity score matching exercise.

Authors	Data Sources	Purpose (Greene et al. 1989)	Description and Q^2 value-added
Shaffer (2012)	Household surveys	Triangulation Development	Propensity score matching drawing on outcome data from household surveys was combined with perceptual information on how respondents 'would have acted in the absence of the program'. The two analytical techniques came to similar results with respect to health and school fee exemptions, thereby bolstering the validity of research results through triangulation.

A3.4 *Defining benefits*

This study compares changes in standard indicators of project impact with those identified by participants in focus group discussion. Accordingly, Q^2 analysis is used to address the metric which should be used to gauge programme success or failure.

Authors	Data sources	Purpose (Greene *et al.* 1989)	Description and Q^2 value-added
De Silva and Gunetilleke (2008)	Focus group discussions Household survey	Complementarity Expansion	Impact results drawing on variables in household survey data, such as access to toilets, water and energy, were compared with impact indicators identified by focus group participants. Satisfaction with changes in the former were off-set by dissatisfaction with such factors as the loss of a quiet rural environment and land devoted to paddy cultivation.

References

Abadie, A. and Imbens, G. (2009). 'Matching on the Estimated Propensity Score', *NBER Working Paper 15301*. Cambridge, M.A.: National Bureau of Economic Research.

Abbott, A. (2001). *Chaos of Disciplines*. Chicago: The University of Chicago Press.

Adams *et al*. (1997). 'Socio-economic Stratification by Wealth Ranking: Is it Valid?', *World Development*, 25(7): 1165–1172.

Adato, M. (2008). 'Combining Survey and Ethnographic Methods to Improve Evaluation of Conditional Cash Transfer Programs', *International Journal of Multiple Research Approaches*, 2(2): 222–236.

Adato, M., Carter, M., and May, J. (2006). 'Exploring Poverty Traps and Social Exclusion in South Africa using Qualitative and Quantitative Data', *Journal of Development Studies*, 42(2): 226–247.

Adato, M., Lund, F., and Mhlongo, P. (2007). 'Methodological Innovations in Research on the Dynamics of Poverty: A Longitudinal Study in KwaZulu-Natal, South Africa', *World Development*, 35(2): 247–263.

Anand, S. and Sen, A. (1997). 'Concepts of Human Development and Poverty: A Multidimensional Perspective', in *Human Development Papers 1997*. New York: United Nations Development Programme, 1–20.

Angrist, J., Imbens, G., and Rubin, D. (1996). 'Identification of Causal Effects Using Instrumental Variables', *Journal of the American Statistical Association*, 91(434): 444–455.

Ayer, A. J. (1959). *Language, Truth, and Logic*. Harmondsworth, UK: Penguin Books, (original work published 1936).

Bamberger, M., Rao, V., and Woolcock, M. (2010). 'Using Mixed Methods in Monitoring and Evaluation. Experiences from International Development', *Policy Research Working Paper 5245*, World Bank, Washington, D.C.

Banerjee, A. and Duflo, E. (2011). *Poor Economics. A Radical Rethinking of the Way to Fight Global Poverty*. New York: Public Affairs.

Barahona, C. and Levy, S. (2007). 'The Best of Both Worlds: Producing National Statistics using Participatory Methods', *World Development*, 35(2): 326–341.

Bardhan, P. and Ray, I. (2006). 'Methodological Approaches to the Question of the Commons', *Economic Development and Cultural Change*, 54(3): 655–676.

Barrett, C. (2003). 'Integrating Qualitative and Quantitative Approaches: Lessons from the Pastoral Risk Management Project', in R. Kanbur (ed.), *Q-squared: qualitative and quantitative poverty appraisal*. Delhi: Permanent Black, 90–96.

Barrett, C. *et al*. (2006). 'Welfare Dynamics in Rural Kenya and Madagascar', *Journal of Development Studies*, *42*(2): 248–277.

Barrientos, A. and Hulme, D. (eds) (2008). *Social Protection for the Poor and the Poorest. Concepts, Policies and Politics*. Basingstoke and New York: Palgrave MacMillan.

Baulch, B. and Davis, P. (2008). 'Poverty Dynamics and Life Trajectories in Rural Bangladesh', *International Journal of Multiple Research Approaches*, *2* (2): 176–190.

Baulch, B. and Hoddinott, J. (eds) (2000). *Economic Mobility and Poverty Dynamics in Developing Countries*. London and Portland: Frank Cass.

Baumgardt, D. (1966). *Bentham and the Ethics of Today*. New York: Octagon Books, Inc.

Bebbington, A. (1999). 'Capitals and Capabilities: A Framework for Analyzing Peasant Viability, Rural Livelihoods and Poverty', *World Development*, *27*(12): 2021–2044.

Beegle, K., Himelein, K., and Ravallion, M. (2009). 'Frame-of-Reference Bias in Subjective Welfare Regressions', *World Bank Policy Research Working Paper No. 4904*, World Bank, Washington, D.C.

Bennett, J. (1971). *Locke, Berkeley, Hume: Central Themes*. Oxford: Oxford University Press.

Bentham, J. (1948). *The Principles of Morals and Legislation*. New York: Haffner Press (original published work 1823).

Bernstein, R.J. (1976). *The Restructuring of Social and Political Theory*. Philadelphia: University of Pennsylvania Press.

Berry, S. (1993). *No Condition is Permanent. The Social Dynamics of Agrarian Change in Sub-Saharan Africa*. Madison, W.I.: The University of Wisconsin Press.

Bevan, P. and Joireman, S. (1997). 'The Perils of Measuring Poverty: Identifying the "Poor" in Rural Ethiopia', *Oxford Development Studies*, *25*(3): 315–343.

Boltvinik, J. (1998). *Poverty Measurement Methods—an Overview*, mimeo, New York City: United Nations Development Programme.

Booth, D., Leach, M. and Tierney, A. (2006). 'Experiencing Poverty in Africa: Perspectives from Anthropology,' *Q-Squared Working Paper No. 25*, Centre for International Studies, University of Toronto, June.

Bourguignon, F. and da Silva, L. (eds) (2003). *The Impact of Economic Policies on Poverty and Income Distribution. Evaluation Techniques and Tools*. Washington, D.C.: World Bank and Oxford University Press.

Brannen, J. (2005). 'Mixed methods Research: A Discussion Paper', *National Centre for Research Methods Review Paper 005*, University of Southampton, Southampton, UK.

Braybrooke, D. (1987). *Philosophy of Social Science*. New Jersey: Prentice-Hall Inc.

Briggs, A. (1961). *Social Thought and Social Action. A Study of the Work of Seebohm Rowntree*. London: Longmans.

Brock, K. and McGee, R. (eds) (2002). *Knowing Poverty: Critical Reflections on Participatory Research and Policy*. London: Earthscan Publications.

Broegaard, E., Freeman, T. and Schwensen, C. (2011). 'Experience from a Phased Mixed-Methods Approach to Impact Evaluation of Danida Support to Rural Transport Infrastructure in Nicaragua', *Journal of Development Effectiveness*, *3*(1): 9–27.

Bryman, A. (1984). 'The Debate about Quantitative and Qualitative Research: A Question of Method or Epistemology?', *The British Journal of Sociology*, *35*(1): 75–92.

Burns, A. and W. Mitchell (1946). *Measuring Business Cycles*. New York: National Bureau of Economic Research.

Caldwell, B. (1982). *Beyond Positivism. Economic Methodology in the Twentieth Century*. London and New York: Routledge.

Camfield, L., Crivello, G., and Woodhead, M. (2009). 'Well-being Research in Developing Countries: Reviewing the Role of Qualitative Methods', *Social Indicators Research*, *90*(1): 5–31.

Campenhout, B. (2006). 'Locally Adapted Poverty Indicators Derived from Participatory Wealth Rankings: A Case of Four Villages in Rural Tanzania', *Journal of African Economies*, *16*(3): 406–438

Carter, M. and Barrett, C. (2006). 'The Economics of Poverty Traps and Persistent Poverty: An Asset-Based Approach', *Journal of Development Studies*, *42*(2): 178–199.

Cartwright, N. (2004). 'Causation: One Word, Many Things', *Philosophy of Science*, *71*(5): 805–819.

Cartwright, N. (2007). *Hunting Causes and Using Them. Approaches in Philosophy and Economics*. Cambridge: Cambridge University Press.

Chalmers, A. (1999). *What is this Thing called Science?* Indianapolis: Hackett Publishing Co. (third edition).

Chambers, R. (1983). *Rural Development. Putting the Last First*. New York City: Longman Scientific and Technical.

Chambers, R. (1988). 'Poverty in India: Concepts, Research and Reality', *IDS Discussion Paper 241*, Institute of Development Studies, University of Sussex.

Chambers, R. (1995). 'Poverty and livelihoods: Whose Reality Counts?', *Environment and Urbanization*, *7*(1): 173–204.

Chambers, R. (2003a). 'The Best of Both Worlds', in R. Kanbur (ed.), *Q-squared: Qualitative and Quantitative Poverty Appraisal*. Delhi: Permanent Black, 35–45.

Chambers, R. (2003b). 'Qualitative Approaches: Self-Criticism and What can be Gained from Quantitative Approaches', in R. Kanbur (ed.), *Q-Squared: Qualitative and Quantitative Methods of Poverty Appraisal*. Delhi: Permanent Black, 28–34.

Christiaensen, L. (2003). 'The Qual-Quant Debate within its Epistemological Context: Some Practical Implications,' in R. Kanbur (ed.), *Q-Squared: Qualitative and Quantitative Methods of Poverty Appraisal*. Delhi: Permanent Black, 114–119.

Christiaensen, L., Hoddinott, J. and Bergeron, G. (2001). 'Comparing Village Characteristics Derived from rapid Appraisals and Household Surveys: A Tale from Northern Mali,' *The Journal of Development Studies*, *37*(3): 1–20.

Cohen, G. (1978). *Karl Marx's Theory of History. A Defence*. Princeton: Princeton University Press.

Collier, P. (2007). *The Bottom Billion*. Oxford: Oxford University Press.

Collins, D. *et al.* (eds) (2009). *Portfolios of the Poor: How the World's Poor Live on $2 a Day*. Princeton and Oxford: Princeton University Press.

Cook, T. (2000). 'Comment. Impact Evaluation: Concepts and Methods', in O. Feinstein and R. Picciotto (eds), *Evaluation and Poverty Reduction*. Washington, D.C.: The World Bank, 76–82.

Creswell, J. *et al.* (2003). 'Advanced Mixed Methods Research Designs', in
A. Tashakkori and C. Teddle (eds), *Handbook of Mixed Methods in Social & Behavioral Research*. Thousand Oaks, C.A.: Sage, 209–240.

Cuong, N. (n.d.). 'Assessing the Impact of Poverty Reduction Programs in Vietnam', Mimeo, Hanoi.

da Corta, L. (2011). 'The Political Economy of Agrarian Change: Dinosaur or Phoenix?', in B. Harriss-White and J. Heyer (eds), *The Comparative Political Economy of Development*. London and New York: Routledge.

Das, J. and Hammer, J. (2005). 'Which Doctor? Combining Vignettes and Item Response to Measure Clinical Competence', *Journal of Development Economics*, *78*(2): 348–383.

Davis, P. and Baulch, B. (2011). 'Parallel Realities: Exploring Poverty Dynamics Using Mixed Methods in Rural Bangladesh', *Journal of Development Studies*, *47*(1): 118–142.

de Kruijk, H. and Rutten, M. (2007). 'Weighting Dimensions of Poverty based on People's Priorities: Constructing a Composite Poverty Index for the Maldives', *Institute for International and Development Economics (IIDE) Discussion Paper 200708–01*, Rotterdam, the Netherlands, August.

de Silva, N. and Gunetilleke, N. (2008). 'On Trying to be Q-Squared: Merging Methods for a Technical Minded Client', *International Journal of Multiple Research Approaches*, *2*(2): 252–265.

de Weerdt, J. (2010). 'Moving out of Poverty in Tanzania: Evidence from Kagera', *Journal of Development Studies*, *46*(2): 331–349.

Deaton, A. (1997). *The Analysis of Household Surveys. A Microeconometric Approach to Development Policy*. Baltimore and London: John Hopkins Press.

Deaton, A. and Grosh, M. (2000). 'Consumption', in M. Grosh and P. Glewwe (eds), *Designing Household Survey Questionnaires for Developing Countries. Lessons from 15 Years of the Living Standards Measurement Study*. Washington, D.C.: The World Bank, 91–133.

Deaton, A. and Zaidi, S. (2002). *'Guidelines of Constructing Consumption Aggregates for Welfare Analysis'*, Mimeo, Princeton University, Princeton, N.J.

Dercon, S. and Shapiro, J. (2007) 'Moving On, Staying Behind, Getting Lost: Lessons on Poverty Mobility from Longitudinal Data', in D. Narayan and P. Petesch (eds), *Moving Out of Poverty. Cross-Disciplinary Perspectives on Mobility*. Washington, D.C.: The World Bank, 77–126.

Devereux, S. (2003). 'Conceptualising Destitution', *IDS Working Paper No. 216*, Institute of Development Studies, University of Sussex, Brighton, UK.

Devereux, S. and Sharp, K. (2006). 'Trends in Poverty and Destitution in Wollo, Ethiopia', *Journal of Development Studies*, *42*(4): 592–610.

Dobb, M. (1973). *Theories of Value and Distribution Since Adam Smith. Ideology and Economic Theory*. Cambridge: Cambridge University Press.

Dow, S. (2004). 'Structured Pluralism', *Journal of Economic Methodology*, *11*(3): 275–290.

Drinkwater, R. (1960). 'Seebohm Rowntree's Contribution to the Study of Poverty', *Advancement of Science*, *16*: 189–196.

Drinkwater, M. (1992). 'Visible Actors and Visible Researchers: Critical Hermeneutics in an Actor-oriented Perspective,' *Sociologia Ruralis*, *32*(4): 367–388.

du Toit, A. (2009). 'Poverty Measurement Blues: Beyond "Q-Squared" Approaches to Understanding Chronic Poverty in South Africa', in T. Addison, D. Hulme, and R. Kanbur (eds), *Poverty Dynamics: Interdisciplinary Perspectives*. Oxford: Oxford University Press, 225–246.

Duflo, E., Glennerster, R. and Kremer, M. (2008). 'Using Randomization in Development Economics Research: A Toolkit', in T. P. Schultz and J. Strauss (eds), *Handbook of Development Economics. Volume 4*. Amsterdam: North Holland, 3895–3962.

Ellis, F. (2000). *Rural Livelihoods and Diversity in Developing Countries*. Oxford: Oxford University Press.

Ellis, F., and Bahiigwa, G. (2003). 'Livelihoods and Rural Poverty Reduction in Uganda', *World Development*, *31*(6): 997–1013.

Ellis, F., and Mdoe, N. (2003). 'Livelihoods and Rural Poverty Reduction in Tanzania', *World Development*, *31*(8): 1367–1384.

Ellis, F., Kutengule, M., and Nyasulu, A. (2003). 'Livelihoods and Rural Poverty Reduction in Malawi', *World Development*, *31*(9): 1495–1510.

Ellis, F., and Freeman, H. (2004). 'Rural Livelihoods and Poverty Reduction Strategies in Four African Countries', *Journal of Development Studies*, *40*(4): 1–30.

Elster, J. (1987). *Sour Grapes. Studies in the Subversion of Rationality*. Cambridge: Cambridge University Press.

Elster, J. (1998). 'A Plea for Mechanisms', in P. Hedström and R. Swedberg (eds), *Social Mechanisms: An Analytical Approach to Social Theory*. Cambridge: Cambridge University Press, 45–73.

Epstein, S. (2007). 'Poverty, Caste and Migration in South India', in D. Narayan and P. Petesch (eds), *Moving Out of Poverty Volume I. Cross-Disciplinary Perspectives on Mobility*. New York: Palgrave MacMillan and the World Bank, 199–226.

Esposito, L, Kebede, B., and Maddox, B. (2012). 'The Value of Literary Practices', *Q-Squared Working Paper No. 59*, Department of International Development Studies, Trent University, Canada.

Fay, B. (1975). *Social theory and Political Practice*. London: George Allen & Unwin Ltd.

Filmer, D. and Pritchett, L. (2001). 'Estimating Wealth Effects without Expenditure Data or Tears: An Application to Educational Enrolments in States of India', *Demography*, *38*(1): 115–132.

Fisher, G. (1992). 'The Development and History of the Poverty Thresholds', *Social Security Bulletin*, *55*(4): 3–14.

Forester, J. (1985). 'Introduction: The Applied Turn in Contemporary Critical Theory', in J. Forester (ed.), *Critical Theory and Public Life*. Cambridge, M.A.: MIT Press, ix–xix.

Francis, E. and Hoddinott, J. (1993). 'Migration and Differentiation in Western Kenya: A Tale of Two Sub-Locations', *Journal of Development Studies*, *30*(1): 115–145.

Franco, S. (2007). 'Poverty in Peru: A Comparison of Different Approaches', in F. Stewart, R. Saith, and B. Harris-White (eds), *Defining Poverty in the Developing World*. New York, N.Y.: Palgrave MacMillan, 160–197.

Frankel, S. and Lehmann, D. (1984). 'Oral Rehydration Therapy: Combining Anthropological and Epidemiological Approaches in the Evaluation of a Papua New Guinea Programme', *Journal of Tropical Medicine and Hygiene, 87*(3): 137–142.

Freeman, H., Ellis, F., and Allison, E. (2004). 'Livelihoods and Rural Poverty Reduction in Kenya. *Development Policy Review'*, *22*(2): 147–173.

George, A. and Bennett, A. (2004). *Case Studies and Theory Development in the Social Sciences*. Cambridge, M.A.: MIT Press.

Giddens, A. (1976). *New Rules of Sociological Method: A Positive Critique of Interpretative Sociologies*. London: Hutchison and Co.

Gilovich, T. and Griffin, D. (2002). 'Introduction—Heuristics and Biases: Then and Now', in T. Gilovich, D. Griffin, and D. Kahneman (eds), *Heuristics and Biases. The Psychology of Intuitive Judgement*. Cambridge: Cambridge University Press, 1–18.

Glennan, S. (2011). 'Mechanisms', in H. Beebee, C. Hitchcock and P. Menzies (eds), *The Oxford Handbook of Causation*. Oxford: Oxford University Press, 315–325.

Glymour, C. (1986). 'Comment. Statistics and Metaphysics', *Journal of the American Statistical Association, 81*(396): 964–966.

Godrey-Smith, P. (2011). 'Causal Pluralism', in H. Beebee, C. Hitchcock, and P. Menzies (eds), *The Oxford Handbook of Causation*. Oxford: Oxford University Press, 326–337.

Gough, I. and McGregor, J. (eds) (2007). *Wellbeing in Developing Countries. From Theory to Research*. Cambridge: Cambridge University Press.

Granovetter, M. (2005) 'The Impact of Social Structure on Economic Outcomes', *Journal of Economic Perspectives, 19*(1): 33–50.

Green, M. (2006). 'Representing Poverty and Attacking Representations: Perspectives on Poverty from Social Anthropology', *Journal of Development Studies, 42*(7): 1108–1129.

Green, M. (2009). 'The Social Distribution of Sanctioned Harm: Thinking through Chronic Poverty, Durable Poverty and Destitution', in T. Addison, D. Hulme and R. Kanbur (eds), *Poverty Dynamics: Interdisciplinary Perspectives*. Oxford: Oxford University Press, 309–327.

Greene, J., Caracelli, V. and Graham, W. (1989). 'Toward a Conceptual Framework for Mixed-Method Evaluation Designs', *Educational Evaluation and Policy Analysis, 11*(3): 255–274.

Grodin, J. (1994). *Introduction to Philosophical Hermeneutics*. New Haven: Yale University Press.

Grootaert, C. and Narayan, D. (2004). 'Local Institutions, Poverty and Household Welfare in Bolivia', *World Development, 32*(7): 1179–1198.

Grosh, M. and Glewwe, P. (1995). 'A Guide to Living Standards Measurement Study Surveys and Their Data Sets,' *Living Standards Measurement Series Working Paper No. 120*, World Bank, Washington D.C.

Grusky, D. and Kanbur, R. (eds) (2006). *Poverty and Inequality*. Stanford: Stanford University Press.

Habermas, J. (1984). *The Theory of Communicative Action. Volume 1: Reason and the Rationalization of Society*. Cambridge: Polity Press.

Habermas, J. (1991). 'Moral Consciousness and Communicative Action,' in *Moral Consciousness and Communicative Action*. Cambridge, M.A.: MIT Press, 116–194.

Hall, N. (2004). 'Two Concepts of Causation', in J. Collins, N. Hall, and L. A. Paul (eds), *Causation and Counterfactuals*. Cambridge, M.A.: MIT Press, 181–203.

Hammersley, M. (1992). *What's Wrong with Ethnography? Methodological Explorations*. London and New York: Routledge.

Harré, R. (1985). *The Philosophies of Science*. Oxford: Oxford University Press (second edition).

Harris, J. (2009). 'Bringing Politics Back into Poverty Analysis: Why Understandings of Social Relations matters More for Policy on Chronic Poverty than Measurement', in T. Addison, D. Hulme, and R. Kanbur (eds), *Poverty Dynamics: Interdisciplinary Perspectives*. Oxford: Oxford University Press, 205–224.

Hargreaves, J. *et al.* (2007). '"Hearing the Voices of the Poor": Assigning Poverty Lines on the Basis of Local Perceptions of Poverty. A Quantitative Analysis of Qualitative Data from Participatory Wealth Ranking in Rural South Africa', *World Development*, 35(2): 212–229.

Haswell, M. (1975). *The Nature of Poverty: Case History of the First Quarter-Century after World War II*. London: MacMillan Publishing.

Haughton, J. and Khandker, S. (2009). *Handbook on Poverty and Inequality*. Washington, D.C.: The World Bank.

Hayati, D., Karami, E., and Slee, B. (2006). 'Combining Qualitative and Quantitative Methods in the Measurement of Rural Poverty: The Case of Iran', *Social Indicators Research*, 75(3): 361–394.

Heckman, J. (2000). 'Comment. Impact Evaluation: Concepts and Methods', in O. Feinstein and R. Picciotto (eds), *Evaluation and Poverty Reduction*. Washington, D.C.: The World Bank, 83–84.

Hedström, P. and Swedberg, R. (eds) (1998). *Social Mechanisms: An Analytical Approach to Social Theory*. Cambridge: Cambridge University Press.

Hentschel, J. (1999). 'Contextuality and Data Collection Methods: A Framework and Application to Health Service Utilisation,' *Journal of Development Studies*, 35(4): 64–94.

Hentschel, J. (2003). 'Integrating the Qual and the Quant: When and Why?', in R. Kanbur (ed.), *Q-squared: Qualitative and Quantitative Poverty Appraisal*. Delhi: Permanent Black, 120–125.

Hill, P. (1977). *Population, Prosperity and Poverty. Rural Kano 1900 and 1970*. Cambridge: Cambridge University Press.

Hitchcock, C. (2002). 'Probabilistic Causation', in E. Zalta (ed.), *The Stanford Encyclopedia of Philosophy*, substanive revision of 6 September [online encyclopedia], <http://plato.stanford.edu/entries/causation-probabilistic/> (accessed 12 June 2008).

Hitchcock, C. (2010). 'Probabilistic Causation', in E. Zalta (ed.), *The Stanford Encyclopedia of Philosophy*, substanive revision of 21 March [online encyclopedia], <http://plato.stanford.edu/entries/causation-probabilistic/> (accessed 15 August 2012).

Holland, P. (1986). 'Statistics and Causal Inference', *Journal of the American Statistical Association*, 81(396): 945–960.

Hoover, K. (1990). 'The Logic of Causal Inference: Econometrics and the Conditional Analysis of Causality', *Economics and Philosophy*, 6(2): 207–234.

Hoover, K. (2008). 'Causality in Economic and Econometrics', in S. Durlauf and L. Blume (eds), *The New Palgrave Dictionary of Economics. Second Edition.* Palgrave Macmillan. [online dictionary], <http://www.dictionaryofeconomics.com/article?id=pde2008_C000569> (accessed 1 September 2012).

Howe, G. and McKay, A. (2007). 'Combining Quantitative and Qualitative Methods in Assessing Chronic Poverty: The Case of Rwanda', *World Development, 35*(2): 197–211.

Howey, R. (1989). *The Rise of the Marginal Utility School 1870–1889.* New York: Columbia University Press.

Hume, D. (1988). *A Treatise of Human Nature*, ed. L. A. Selby-Bigge. Oxford: Clarendon Press (original work published 1740).

Hume, D. (1902). *Enquiry Concerning the Principles of Morals*, ed. L. A. Selby-Bigge. Oxford: Clarendon Press (second edition; original work published 1777).

Iliffe, J. (1987). *The African Poor.* Cambridge: Cambridge University Press.

International Institute for Environment and Development (IIED) (1992). 'Special Issue on Applications of Wealth Ranking', *RRA Notes No. 15*, IIED, London.

Jalan, J. and Ravallion, M. (2000). 'Is Transient Poverty Different? Evidence for Rural China', *Journal of Development Studies, 36* (2): 82–99.

Jevons W. (1871). *The Theory of Political Economy.* London and New York: MacMillan.

Jodha, N. (1988). 'Poverty Debate in India: A Minority View', *Economic and Political Weekly*, 23 (45/47), November: 2421–2428.

Johnson, G. (n.d.). 'A long Trail of Evidence links Cigarette Smoking to Cancer', <http://txtwriter.com/Onscience/Articles/smokingcancer2.html> (accessed 17 August 2009).

Joint Donor Report (JDR) (2004). *Vietnam Development Report 2004. Poverty.* Asian Development Bank, the Australian Agency for International Development, Department for International Development (UK), the German Agency for Development Co-operation, Japan International Cooperation Agency, Save the Children (UK), United Nations Development Programme and the World Bank, Hanoi.

Jolliffe, D. (2001). 'Measuring Absolute and Relative Poverty: The Sensitivity of Estimated Household Consumption to Survey Design,' *Journal of Economic and Social Measurement, 27*(1/2): 1–23.

Kahneman, D. (2011). *Thinking, Fast and Slow.* Toronto: Doubleday Canada.

Kanbur, R. (2001). 'Economic Policy, Distribution and Poverty: The Nature of Disagreements', *World Development, 29*(6): 1083–1094.

Kanbur, R. (2002). 'Economics, Social Science and Development', *World Development, 30*(3): 477–486.

Kanbur, R. (ed.) (2003). *Q-squared: Qualitative and Quantitative Poverty Appraisal.* Delhi: Permanent Black.

Kanbur, R. (2003). 'Q-squared? A Commentary on Qualitative and Quantitative Poverty Appraisal', in R. Kanbur (ed.), *Q-squared: Qualitative and Quantitative Poverty Appraisal.* Delhi: Permanent Black, 1–21.

Kanbur, R. and Riles, A. (2006). 'And Never the Twain Shall Meet? An Exchange on the Strengths and Weaknesses of Anthropology and Economics in Analyzing the Commons,' *Q-Squared Working Paper No. 22*, Centre for International Studies, University of Toronto.

Kanbur, R. and Shaffer, P. (eds) (2007a). 'Special Issue: Experiences of Combining Qualitative and Quantitative Approaches in Poverty Analysis', *World Development, 35*(2): 183–353.

Kanbur, R. and Shaffer, P. (2007b). 'Epistemology, Normative Theory and Poverty Analysis: Implications for Q-Squared in Practice', *World Development, 35*(2): 183–196.

Kapoor, I. (2002). 'The Devil's in the Theory: A Critical Assessment of Robert Chambers' Work on Participatory Development', *Third World Quarterly, 23*(1): 101–107.

Kebede, B. (2009). 'Community Wealth Ranking and Household Surveys: An Integrative Approach', *Journal of Development Studies, 45*(10): 1731–1746.

King, G., Murray, C., Salomon, J., and Tandon, A. (2004). 'Enhancing the Validity and Cross-Cultural Comparability of Measurement in Survey Research', *American Political Science Review, 98*(1): 191–207.

King, G. and Wand, J. (2007). 'Comparing Incomparable Survey Responses: Evaluating and Selecting Anchoring Vignettes', *Political Analysis, 15*(1): 46–66.

Koopmans, T. (1947). 'Measurement without Theory', *Review of Economic Statistics, 29*: 161–172.

Krishna, A. (2010a). 'Who Became Poor, Who Escaped Poverty and Why? Developing and Using a Retrospective Methodology in Five Countries', *Journal of Policy Analysis and Management, 29*(2): 351–372.

Krishna, A. (2010b). *One Illness Away. Why People Become Poor and How They Escape Poverty.* Oxford: Oxford University Press.

Krishna, A. *et al.* (2006a). 'Escaping Poverty and Becoming Poor in 36 Villages of Central and Western Uganda', *Journal of Development Studies, 42*(2): 346–370.

Krishna, A. *et al.* (2006b). 'Fixing the Hole in the Bucket: Household Poverty Dynamics in the Peruvian Andes', *Development and Change, 37*(5): 997–1021.

Krishna, A. and Lecy, D. (2008). 'The Balance of All Things: Explaining Household Poverty Dynamics in 50 Villages of Gujarat, India', *International Journal of Multiple Research Approaches, 2*(2): 160–175.

Kristensen, N. and Johansson, E. (2008). 'New Evidence on Cross-Country Differences in Job Satisfaction using Vignettes,' *Labor Economics, 15*(1): 96–117.

Lanjouw, P and Stern, N. (eds) (1998). *Economic Development in Palanpur over Five Decades.* Oxford: Clarendon Press.

Lawson, D., Hulme, D. and Muwonge, J. (2008). 'Combining Quantitative and Qualitative Research to Further our Understanding of Poverty Dynamics: Some Methodological Considerations', *International Journal of Multiple Research Approaches, 2*(2): 191–204.

Layard, R. (2005). *Happiness: Lessons from a New Science.* London: Allen Lane.

Levine, S. and Roberts, B. (2008). 'Combined Methods in Poverty Analysis: Experiences from Namibia', *International Journal of Multiple Research Approaches, 2*(2): 205–221.

Lewis, D. (1973). *Counterfactuals.* Oxford: Blackwell.

References

Lipton, M. (1970). 'Interdisciplinary Studies in less Developed Countries', *Journal of Development Studies, 7*(1): 5–18.

Lipton, M. (1983). 'Poverty, Undernutrition and Hunger', *World Bank Staff Working Papers No. 597,* World Bank, Washington D.C.

Lipton, M. (1988). 'The Poor and the Poorest', *World Bank Discussion Paper No. 25,* World Bank, Washington, D.C.

Lipton, M. (1992). 'Economics and Anthropology: Grounding Models in Relationships', *World Development 20*(10): 1541–1546.

Lipton, P. (2001). 'Empiricism, History of', *International Encyclopedia of the Social & Behavioral Sciences,* Elsevier Science Ltd, Amsterdam, 4481–4485.

Little, D. (1991). *Varieties of Social Explanation.* Boulder: Westview Press.

Little, D. (1998). *Microfoundations, Method and Causation.* New Brunswick: Transaction Publishers.

Little, P. *et al.* (2006). '"Moving in Place": Drought and Poverty Dynamics in South Wollo, Ethiopia', *Journal of Development Studies, 42*(2): 200–225.

Lokshin, M., Umapathi, N., and Paternostro, S. (2006). 'Robustness of Subjective Welfare Analysis in a Poor Developing Country: Madagascar 2001', *Journal of Development Studies, 42*(4): 559–591.

Lu, C. (2010). 'Who is Poor in China? A Comparison of Alternative Approaches to Poverty Assessment in Rural Yunnan', *Journal of Peasant Studies, 37*(2): 407–428.

Lu, C. (2011). *Poverty and Development in China. Alternative Approaches to Poverty Assessment.* New York: Routledge.

Machamer, P., Darden, L., and Craver, C. (2000). 'Thinking about Mechanisms', *Philosophy of Science, 67*(1): 1–25.

MacIntyre, A. (2007). *After Virtue.* Notre Dame: University of Notre Dame Press (third edition; original work published 1981).

Mahoney, J. (2001). 'Beyond Correlational Analysis: Recent Innovations in Theory and Method', *Sociological Forum, 16*(3): 575–593.

Maluccio, J., Haddad, L. and May, J. (2000). 'Social Capital and Income Generation in South Africa 1993–1998', *Journal of Development Studies, 36*(6): 54–81.

Maluccio, J. and Flores, R. (2005). 'Impact Evaluation of a Conditional Cash Transfer Program: The Nicaraguan Red de Protección Social', *Research Report 141,* International Food Policy Research Institute, Washington, D.C.

Marsh, C. (1979). 'Problems with Surveys: Method or Epistemology?', *Sociology, 13*(2): 293–305.

Mathison, S. (1988). 'Why Triangulate?', *Educational Researcher, 17*(2): 13–17.

Mayoux, L. and Chambers, R. (2005). 'Reversing the Paradigm: Quantification, Participatory Methods and Pro-Poor Impact Assessment', *Journal of International Development, 17*(2): 271–298.

McCollum E. (1957). *A History of Nutrition. The Sequence of Ideas in Nutrition Investigations.* Boston: Houghton Mifflin Co.

McGee, R. (2004). 'Constructing Poverty Trends in Uganda: A Multidisciplinary Perspective', *Development and Change, 35* (3): 499–523.

McGillivray, M. (2007). *Human Well-Being: Concept and Measurement.* Basingstoke: Palgrave-MacMillan.

Menzies, P. (2008). 'Counterfactual Theories of Causation', in E. Zalta (ed.), *The Stanford Encyclopedia of Philosophy,* substantive revision of 30 March [online encyclopedia] <http://plato.stanford.edu/entries/causation-counterfactual/> (Accessed 30 June 2008).

Moore, M., Choudhary, M. and Singh, N. (1998). 'How can *We* Know What *They* Want? Understanding Local Perceptions of Poverty and Ill-being in Asia,' *IDS Working Paper 80,* Institute of Development Studies, University of Sussex, Brighton, UK.

Morewedge, D. (2012). 'It was a Most Unusual Time: How memory Bias Engenders Nostalgic Preferences', *Journal of Behavioral Decision Making*, published online in Wiley online Library DOI:10.1002/bdm.1767.

Morgan, M. (1990). *The History of Econometric Ideas.* Cambridge: Cambridge University Press.

Morse, J. (1991). 'Approaches to Qualitative-Quantitative Methodological Triangulation,' *Nursing Research, 40*(2): 120–123.

Morse, J. (2003). 'Principles of Mixed Method and Multimethod Research Design,' in A. Tashakkori and C. Teddle (eds), *Handbook of Mixed Methods in Social & Behavioral Research.* Sage: Thousand Oaks, C.A., 189–208.

Moser, C. (1998). 'The Asset Vulnerability Framework: Reassessing Urban Poverty Reduction Strategies', *World Development, 26*(1): 1–19.

Mosse, D. (2006). 'Collective Action, Common Property and Social Capital in India: An Anthropological Commentary', *Economic Development and Cultural Change, 54*(3): 695–724.

Nagel, E. (1961). *The Structure of Science.* New York and Burlingame: Harcourt, Brace & World, Inc.

Narayan, D. (ed) (2009). *Moving out of Poverty Volume 3. The Promise of Empowerment and Democracy in India.* Washington, D.C.: The World Bank and Palgrave Macmillan.

Narayan, D. *et al.* (2002). *Can Anyone Hear Us? Voices of the Poor.* Oxford: Oxford University Press.

Narayan, D., Pritchett, L., and Kapoor, S. (2009). *Moving Out of Poverty Volume 2. Success from the Bottom Up.* Washington, D.C.: The World Bank and Palgrave Macmillan.

Noxon, J. (1973). *Hume's Philosophical Development: A Study of his Methods.* Oxford: Clarendon Press.

O'Laughlin, B. (2004). 'Book Reviews', *Development and Change, 35*(2): 385–392

Orshansky, M. (1965). 'Counting the Poor: Another look at the Poverty Profile', *Social Security Bulletin, 28*(1): 1–29.

Osmani, S. (ed) (1992). *Nutrition and Poverty.* Oxford: Clarendon Press.

Pawson, R. (2002). 'Evidence-based Policy: The Promise of "Realistic" Synthesis', *Evaluation, 8*(3): 340–358.

Pawson, R. and Tilley, N. (1997). *Realistic Evaluation.* London: Sage.

Payne, P. and Lipton, M. (1994). 'How Third World Rural Households Adapt to Dietary Energy Stress: The Evidence and Issues', *IFPRI Food Policy Review 2,* International Food Policy Research Institute, Washington, D.C.

References

Pickel, A. (2004). 'Systems and Mechanisms. A Symposium on Mario Bunge's Philosophy of Social Science', *Philosophy of Social Sciences*, 34(2): 169–181.

Pincus, J. and Sender, J. (2008). 'Quantifying Poverty in Vietnam: Who Counts', *Journal of Vietnamese Studies*, 3(1): 108–150.

Place, F., Adato, M. and Hebinck, P. (2007). 'Understanding Rural Poverty and Investment in Agriculture: An Assessment of Integrated Qualitative and Quantitative Research in Western Kenya', *World Development*, 35(2): 312–325.

Plamenatz J. (1958). *The English Utilitarians*. Oxford: Basil Blackwell.

Popper, K. (1959). *The Logic of Scientific Discovery*. London: Hutchinson.

Poteete, A., Janssen, M. and Ostrom, E. (2010). *Working Together: Collective Action, the Commons, and Multiple Methods in Practice*. Princeton and Oxford: Princeton University Press.

Pradhan, M. and Ravallion, M. (2000). 'Measuring Poverty using Qualitative Perceptions of Consumption Adequacy', *The Review of Economics and Statistics*, 82(3): 462–471.

Putnam, H. (1981). *Reason, Truth and History*. Cambridge: Cambridge University Press.

Quisumbing, A. (2011). 'Poverty Transitions, Shocks and Consumption in Rural Bangladesh, 1996–97 to 2006–07', in B. Baulch (ed.), *Why Poverty Persists. Poverty Dynamics in Asia and Africa*. Cheltenham: Edward Elgar Publishing, 29–64.

Rahnema, M. (1991). 'Global Poverty: A Pauperising Myth', *Interculture*, 24(2): 4–51.

Rallis, S. and Rossman, G. (2003). 'Mixed Methods in Evaluation Contexts: A Pragmatic Framework,' in A. Tashakkori and C. Teddle (eds), *Handbook of Mixed Methods in Social & Behavioral Research*. Sage: Thousand Oaks, C.A., 491–512.

Rand, J. (2010). 'Evaluating the Employment Generating Impact of Rural Roads in Nicaragua', *Journal of Development Effectiveness*, 3(1): 28–43.

Rao, V. (2002). 'Experiments in "Participatory Econometrics"', *Economic and Political Weekly*, 18 May: 1887–1891.

Rao, V. (2003). 'Experiments with "Participatory Econometrics" in India: Can Conversation take the Con out of Econometrics?', in R. Kanbur (ed.), *Q-squared: qualitative and quantitative poverty appraisal*. Delhi: Permanent Black, 103–113.

Rao, V. *et al.* (2003). 'Sex Workers and the Cost of Safe Sex: The Compensating Differential for Condom Use among Calcutta Prostitutes', *Journal of Development Economics*, 71(2): 585–603.

Rao, V. and Woolcock, M. (2003). 'Integrating Qualitative and Quantitative Approaches in Program Evaluation', in F. Bourguignon and L. da Silva (eds), *The Impact of Economic Policies on Poverty and Income Distribution. Evaluation Techniques and Tools*. Washington, D.C.: The World Bank and Oxford University Press, 165–190.

Rao, V. and Ibáñez, M. (2005). 'The Social Impact of Social Funds in Jamaica: A "Participatory Econometric" Analysis of Targeting, Collective Action, and Participation in Community-Driven Development', *Journal of Development Studies*, 41(5): 788–838.

Ravallion, M. (1994). *Poverty Comparisons. Fundamentals of Pure and Applied Economics*. Chur, Switzerland: Harwood Academic Publishers.

Ravallion, M. (2001). 'The Mystery of the Vanishing Benefits: An Introduction to Impact Evaluation', *The World Bank Economic Review, 15*(1): 115–140.

Ravallion, M. (2008). 'Evaluating Anti-Poverty Programs', in T. P. Schultz and J. Strauss (eds), *Handbook of Development Economics. Volume 4.* Amsterdam: North Holland, 3787–3846.

Ravallion, M. and Bidani, B. (1994). 'How Robust is a Poverty Profile?', *World Bank Economic Review, 8*(1): 75–102.

Rehg, W. (1994). *Insight and Solidarity. A Study in the Discourse Ethics of Jürgen Habermas.* Berkeley: University of California Press.

Reichenbach, H. (1956). *The Direction of Time.* Berkeley and Los Angeles: University of California Press.

Republic of Rwanda (2001). *Participatory Poverty Assessment.* Ministry of Finance and Economic Planning, National Poverty Reduction Program, Kigali, October.

Robbins, L. (1962). *An Essay on the Nature and Significance of Economic Science.* London: MacMillan and Co. Ltd. (second edition; original work published 1936).

Roche, C. (1999). *Impact Assessment for Development Agencies.* Oxford: Oxfam Publications.

Roth, P. (1987). *Meaning and Method in the Social Sciences. A Case for Methodological Pluralism.* Ithaca: Cornell University Press.

Rowntree, S. (1980). *Poverty: A Study of Town Life.* New York and London: Garland (original work published 1901).

Rowntree, S. (1941). *Poverty and Progress.* London: Longmans.

Rubin, D. B. (1974). 'Estimating Causal Effects on Treatments in Randomized and Nonrandomized Studies', *Journal of Educational Psychology, 66*(5): 688–701.

Ruggeri Laderchi, C., Saith, R., and Stewart, F. (2003). 'Does it Matter that We do not Agree on the Definition of Poverty', *Oxford Development Studies, 31*(3): 243–274.

Russell, B. (1952). *The Problems of Philosophy.* Oxford: Oxford University Press (original work published 1912).

Sachs, J. (2005). *The End of Poverty.* New York: The Penguin Press.

Sahn, D. and Stifel, D. (2003). 'Exploring Alternative Measures of Welfare in the Absence of Expenditure Data', *Review of Income and Wealth, 49*(4): 463–489.

Saith, R. (2007). 'Poverty in India: A Comparison of Different Approaches', in F. Stewart, R. Saith and B. Harris-White (eds), *Defining Poverty in the Developing World.* New York: Palgrave MacMillan, 114–159.

Salomon, J., Tandon, A. and Murray, C. (2001). 'Using Vignettes to Improve Cross-Population Comparability of Health Surveys: Concepts, Design, and Evaluation Techniques', *Global Programme on Evidence for Health Policy Discussion Paper No. 41*, World Health Organisation, Geneva.

Samuelson, P. (1966). 'A Note on the Pure Theory of Consumer's Behavior', in J. Stiglitz (ed.), *The Collected Scientific Papers of Paul A. Samuelson, Volume 1.* Cambridge, M.A.: MIT Press (original work published 1938), 3–13.

Samuelson, P. (1974). 'Complementarity: An Essay on the 40th Anniversary of the Hicks-Allen Revolution in Demand Theory', *Journal of Economic Literature, 12*(4): 1255–1289.

Sayer, A. (1984). *Method in Social Science. A Realist Approach.* London: Hutchinson.

Schaffer, J. (2008). 'The Metaphysics of Causation', in E. Zalta (ed.), *The Stanford Encyclopedia of Philosophy*, [online encyclopedia], <http://plato.stanford.edu/archives/fall2008/entries/causation-metaphysics/> (Accessed 2 July 2008).

Scoones, I. (1995). 'Investigating Difference: Applications of Wealth Ranking and Household Survey Approaches among Farming Households in Southern Zimbabwe,' *Development and Change, 26*(1): 67–88.

Scoones, I. (1998). 'Sustainable Rural Livelihoods: A Framework for Analysis', *IDS Working Paper No. 72*, Institute of Development Studies, University of Sussex, Brighton, UK.

Scoones, I. (2009). 'Livelihoods Perspectives and Rural Development', *Journal of Peasant Studies, 36*(1): 171–196.

Scott, C. and Amenuvegbe, B. (1990). 'Effect of Recall Duration on Reporting of Household Expenditure: An Experimental Study in Ghana,' *Social Dimensions of Adjustment (SDA) Working Paper No. 6*, World Bank, Washington, D.C.

Scriven, M. (2008). 'A Summary Evaluation of RCT Methodology: An Alternative Approach to Causal Research', *Journal of Multidisciplinary Evaluation, 5*(9): 11–24.

Seeley, J. *et al.* (2008). 'Using In-depth Qualitative Results Regarding the Impact of HIV and AIDS on Households in Rural Uganda,' *Social Science and Medicine, 67*(9): 1434–1446.

Sen, A. (1981). *Poverty and Famines. An Essay on Entitlement and Deprivation.* Oxford: Clarendon Press.

Sen, A. (1983). 'Poor, Relatively Speaking', *Oxford Economic Papers, 35*(2): 153–169.

Sen, A. (1999). *Development as Freedom.* New York: Anchor Books.

Sen, A. (2002). 'Health: Perception versus Observation', *British Medical Journal, 325* (7342), 13 April: 860–861.

Shaffer, P. (1998). 'Gender, Poverty, and Deprivation: Evidence from the Republic of Guinea. *World Development', 26*(12): 2119–2135.

Shaffer, P. (2002). 'Poverty Naturalised: Implications for Gender', *Feminist Economics* 8(3): 55–75.

Shaffer, P. (2005). 'Assumptions Matter: Reflections on the Kanbur Typology', *Focaal—European Journal of Anthropology, 45*(1): 18–32.

Shaffer, P. (2008). 'New Thinking on Poverty: Implications for Globalisation and Poverty Reduction Strategies', *Real World Economics Review, 47*(3): 192–231 [online journal], <http://paecon.net/PAEReview/issue47/Shaffer47.pdf>.

Shaffer, P. (2011). 'Against Excessive Rhetoric in Impact Assessment: Overstating the Case for Randomised Controlled Experiments', *Journal of Development Studies, 47*(11): 1619–1635.

Shaffer, P. (2012). 'Beneath the "Methods Debate" in Impact Assessment: Baring Assumptions of a Mixed Methods Impact Assessment in Vietnam', *Journal of Development Effectiveness, 4*(1): 134–150.

Shaffer, P. (forthcoming). 'Ten Years of Q-Squared. Implications for Understanding and Explaining Poverty', *World Development.*

Shaffer, P. *et al.* (eds) (2008). 'Introduction to Q-Squared in Policy: The Use of Qualitative and Quantitative Methods of Poverty Analysis in Decision-Making', *International Journal of Multiple Research Approaches, 2*(2): 134–144.

Sharp, K. (2007). 'Squaring the "Q"s? Methodological Reflections on a Study of Destitution in Ethiopia', *World Development, 35*(2): 264–280.

Sharp, K. and Devereux, S. (2004). 'Destitution in Wollo (Ethiopia): Chronic Poverty as a Crisis of Household and Community Livelihoods', *Journal of Human Development, 5*(2): 227–247.

Simon, H. (1953). 'Causal Order and Identifiability', in W. Hood and T. Koopmans (eds), *Studies in Econometric Method. Cowles Commission Monograph 14*. New Haven: Yale University Press, 49–74.

Sinha, S., Lipton, M. and Yaqub, S. (2002). 'Poverty and "Damaging Fluctuations": How do they Relate?', *Journal of Asian and African Studies, 37*(2): 186–243.

Steel, D. (2011). 'Causality, Causal Models and Social Mechanisms', in I. Jarvie and J. Zamora-Bonilla (eds), *The SAGE Handbook of the Philosophy of Social Sciences*. London: Sage Publications, 288–304.

Stewart, F., Saith, R and Harris-White, B. (eds) (2007). *Defining Poverty in the Developing World*. New York: Palgrave MacMillan.

Stewart, F. *et al.* (2007). 'Alternative Realities? Different Concepts of Poverty, their Empirical Consequences and Policy Implications: Overview and Conclusions', in F. Stewart, R. Saith, and B. Harris-White (eds), *Defining Poverty in the Developing World*. New York: Palgrave MacMillan.

Sudman, S., Bradburn, N. and Schwartz, N. (1996). *Thinking About Answers: The Application of Cognitive Processes to Survey Methodology*. San Francisco: Jossey-Bass Publishers.

Suppes, F. (1970). *A Probabilistic Theory of Causality*. Amsterdam: North-Holland Publications.

Suppes, F. (ed.) (1974). *The Structure of Scientific Theories*. Urbana: The University of Illinois Press.

Takasaki, Y., Barham, B. and Coomes, O. (2000). 'Rapid Rural Appraisal in Humid Tropical Forests: An Asset Possession-Based Approach and Validation Methods for Wealth Assessment Among Forest Peasant Households', *World Development, 28*(11): 1961–1977.

Tashakkori, A. and Teddle, C. (eds) (2003). *Handbook of Mixed Methods in Social & Behavioral Research*. Sage: Thousand Oaks, C.A.

Tashakkori, A. and Teddle, C. (2003a). 'Major Issues and Controversies in the use of Mixed Methods in the Social and Behavioral Sciences', in A. Tashakkori and C. Teddle (eds), *Handbook of Mixed Methods in Social & Behavioral Research*. Sage: Thousand Oaks, C.A., 3–50.

Tashakkori, A. and Teddle, C. (2003b). 'The Past and Future of Mixed Method Research: From Data Triangulation to Mixed Model Designs', in A. Tashakkori and C. Teddle (eds), *Handbook of Mixed Methods in Social & Behavioral Research*. Sage: Thousand Oaks, C.A., 671–701.

Tashakkori, A. and Teddle, C. (eds) (2010). *SAGE Handbook of Mixed Methods in Social & Behavioral Research*. Sage: Thousand Oaks, C.A. (second edition).

Taylor, C. (1985). 'Interpretation and the Science of Man', in C. Taylor (ed), *Philosophy and the Human Sciences*. Cambridge: Cambridge University Press (original work published 1971), 15–57.

Taylor, C. and Pye, O. (1966). *Foundations of Nutrition*. New York: The MacMillan Company (sixth edition).

Temu, A. and Due, J. (2000). 'Participatory Appraisal Approaches versus Sample Survey Data collection: A Case of Smallholder Farmers Well-being Ranking in Njombe District, Tanzania', *Journal of African Economies, 9*(1): 44–62.

Thorbecke, E. (2003). 'Tensions, Complementarities and Possible Convergence between the Qualitative and Quantitative Approaches to Poverty Assessment,' in R. Kanbur (ed.), *Q-squared: Qualitative and Quantitative Poverty Appraisal*. Delhi: Permanent Black, 164–168.

Tourangeau, R., Rips, R. and Rasinski, K. (2000). *The Psychology of Survey Response*. Cambridge: Cambridge University Press.

Townsend. P. (1979). *Poverty in the United Kingdom. A Survey of Household Resources and Standards of Living*. London: Penguin Books.

Tucker, B. *et al.* (2011). 'When the Wealthy are Poor: Poverty Explanations and Local Perspectives in Southwestern Madagascar', *American Anthropologist, 113*(2): 291–305.

United Nations Department of Economic and Social Affairs (UNDESA) (2005). 'Household Sample Surveys in Developing and Transition Countries', *Studies in Methods, Series F No. 96*, United Nations, New York.

Weiss, C. (2000). 'Theory-based Evaluation: Theories of Change for Poverty Reduction Strategies', in O. Feinstein and R. Picciotto (eds), *Evaluation and Poverty Reduction*. Washington, D.C.: The World Bank, 83–84.

White, H. (2008). 'Of Probits and Participation: The Use of Mixed Methods in Quantitative Impact Evaluation', *IDS Bulletin, 39*(1): 98–109.

White, H. (2009a). 'Some Reflections on Current Debates in Impact Evaluation', *International Initiative for Impact Evaluation Working Paper No. 1*, International Initiative for Impact Evaluation, New Delhi, India.

White, H. (2009b). 'Theory-based Impact Evaluation: Principles and Practice', *International Initiative for Impact Evaluation Working Paper No. 3*, International Initiative for Impact Evaluation, New Delhi, India.

White, H. (2011). 'Achieving High-Quality Impact Evaluation through Mixed Methods: The Case of Infrastructure', *Journal of Development Effectiveness, 3*(1): 131–144.

Whitehead, A. (2002). 'Tracking Livelihood Change: Theoretical, Methodological and Empirical Perspectives from North-East Ghana', *Journal of Southern African Studies, 28*(3): 575–598.

Whitehead, A. (2006). 'Persistent Poverty in North East Ghana', *Journal of Development Studies, 42*(2): 278–300.

Wodon, Q. (2007). 'Is there a Divergence between Objective and Subjective Perceptions of Poverty Trends? Evidence from West and Central Africa', *Poverty Data, Measurement and Policy Special Expanded Edition No. 282*, October, World Bank, Washington, D.C.

Woldehanna, T *et al.* (2005). 'Gender Labour, Gender Inequality and Rural/Urban Disparities: How Can Ethiopia's National Development Strategies be Revised to Address Negative Spill-Over Impacts on Child Education and Wellbeing?', *Young Lives Working Paper No. 20*, Young Lives, Save the Children UK, London.

Woldehanna, T., Jones, N., and Tefera, B. (2008). 'The Invisibility of Children's Paid and Unpaid Work. Implication for Ethiopia's National Poverty Reduction Policy', *Childhood*, *15*(2): 177–201.

Wood, G. (2003). 'Staying Secure, Staying Poor: The "Faustian Bargain"', *World Development*, *31*(3): 455–471.

Woodcock, A. *et al.* (2009). 'Validation of the WEDQoL-Goals-Thailand Measure: Culture-Specific Individualised Quality of Life', *Social Indicators Research*, *94*(1): 135–171.

Wright, S. and Nelson, N. (1995). 'Participatory Research and Participant Observation', in N. Nelson and S. Wright (eds), *Power and Participatory Development*. London: Intermediate Technology Publications, 43–59.

Index

Index